U0115529

三幕舞台劇

# 飛機失事以後

姜龍昭著·蔣娉譯

國立中央圖書館出版品預行編目資料

飛機失事以後：三幕舞台劇 = AFTER THE PLANE
CRASH : an original play / 姜龍昭著 ; 蔣
娉譯. -- 初版. -- 臺北市：文史哲，民81
面；　公分.
ISBN 957-547-128-8(平裝)

854.6　　　　　　　　　　　　　81003262

飛機失事以後

著　者：姜　　　龍　　　昭
出版者：文　史　哲　出　版　社
登記證字號：行政院新聞局局版臺業字五三三七號
發行人：彭　　　正　　　雄
發行所：文　史　哲　出　版　社
印刷者：文　史　哲　出　版　社
　　　　台北市羅斯福路一段七十二巷四號
　　　　郵撥〇五一二八八一二彭正雄帳戶
　　　　電話：三　五　一　一　〇　二　八

實價新台幣二四〇元

中華民國八十一年七月初版

# 吳 序

本劇的主要人物桑炳成，是一個社會上受人尊敬的大慈善家，近年來，他經營的貿易公司發了不少財，一些慈善機關的人，上門向他募捐，他總是「有求必應」，「出手大方」。他常說：「為善最樂，做好事，是每一個人的責任。」

可是，有時候，一些至親好友，來請求他幫忙，為一些不法的行為，去向人關說，以求打通關節，則為他斷然拒絕。他告訴來求他的人說：「做人一定要做得正，在社會上，才能受人尊敬，被人看得起。」

因為他是一家貿易公司的董事長，當然也希望他的兒子，將來能繼承他的事業，因此，他常對他的兒子德正說：「德正，我告訴你，要做一個成功的總經理，必先要做好『認人』這件工作，……認識一個人，不是簡單的一件事。因為，人會偽裝、做假；表面和實際，往往並不相符。壞人的臉上，往往寫的是個『好』字。有些『偽』君子戴上了面具，跟真君子沒有兩樣……」

從上述的簡介對白中，我們看出劇作家姜龍昭塑造的桑炳成，是一個喜愛做善事，却又正直、精

明能幹、受人尊敬的「大好人」。但是，當桑炳成所搭乘的飛機，突然失事，因空難而喪亡以後，卻爆發了一些他生前別人所不知道的秘密。

他的女兒德芬，在大學讀書的同學們，看了報上的報導，才知道，他生前所捐獻的，原來都是些「黑心」賺來的「不義之財」，他們拿著報紙，向德芬追問真相，使她羞愧得無地自容，她跪在父親的遺像前，哭著說：

「爸，……你究竟是怎樣的一個人？是大慈善家？還是個偽君子？爸，……你怎麼不說話呢！……『罪惡』不是可以用『捐獻』來洗刷乾淨的，……『名譽』也不是可以用『金錢』來購買裝飾的！……這些道理，你都不知道嗎？……爸……你留給我們的，不是『榮譽』，是『恥辱』。……永遠洗不清的『恥辱』！……我恨你，……恨你……竟然是我的父親！」

「飛機失事以後」，我認為是一齣非常能反映這個時代脈動的好劇本！是一部好的舞臺劇的文學創作。

我相信，沒有豐富的人生體念，沒有足夠的編劇經驗，沒有愛世醒俗的心懷，是絕不可能寫作出這樣深邃精闢的作品。

我認識龍昭先生，近卅年，他多年來擔任中華民國編劇學會的秘書長，從事劇本的創作，已有四十多年的歷史，是一位多產的劇作家，他不但編寫舞臺劇本，也編寫電視劇本、廣播劇本、和電影劇本，每一類的劇本，在演出時，都曾為他帶來不少的喝彩及掌聲。近四十多年來，他得獎的次數，也

二

保有最高的記錄。

　　近年來，他特別專心從事舞臺劇本的創作，在正統舞臺劇的寫作方式及技巧方面，強化了傳統的優點，並加強了新的創意，作品的內涵，充滿了美與善的號召，在現代戲劇寫作方式紛然雜陳的情況下，我覺得尤為難能可貴。

　　據我所知，過去，他的劇本，曾先後在菲律賓、馬來西亞、香港……等地正式公演，頗受各地文友及觀眾的欣賞與喜愛。也有些作品，曾被改編搬上銀幕及螢光幕。最近，他編寫的「淚水的沉思」與「飛機失事以後」，能被譯成英文出版，更是國內劇作家少有的殊榮。

　　本劇是他民國八十年最新的創作，我有幸能先拜讀了原稿，衷心盼望它⋯能引起國內國外戲劇界的重視與關注，更希望能在海內外的舞臺上，看到它不同語言的演出。寫此簡介，表示我的賀意與祝福。

吳若　八十一年文藝節前夕，臺北市

# 黃　序

翻開一本中國戲劇史，便可以發現近百年來的舞臺劇。其興也早，其勢也壯，但却始終受到西洋的影響。

我國舞臺劇，以前稱爲話劇，可以上溯到民國紀元前五年（一九〇七年），在東京的一批留日學生曾孝谷、李叔同、謝抗白等，組織了「春柳社」，爲了賑濟國內徐淮水災，演出了改編法國小仲馬（Dumas fils）的「茶花女遺事」（Camille），後來又演出美國女作家斯托（H. B. Stowe）的小說「黑奴籲天錄」（Uncle Tom's Cabin）。這兩個改編的劇本，都採自大翻譯家林琴南的譯著，使國人接受了一種新舞臺藝術，足見翻譯，帶動了一個時代，功不可沒。這也是我國舞臺劇的濫觴。

到了民國八年五四運動以後，爲了提倡新文藝與介紹新思潮，翻譯工作風起雲湧，翻譯外國的劇本極多，像挪威的易卜生（Henrik Ibsen），法國的莫里哀（Moliere），英國的王爾德（Oscar Wilde）、蕭伯納（G. B. Shaw）·德國的席勒（J. C. F. von Schiller）·俄國的戈果里（Gogol）··比利時的梅特靈克（Maeterlinck）等等。

四

由於舉世的戲劇大家的作品，都能透過翻譯而薈萃於中土，使國人領悟了舞臺劇寫作的藝術，終而有了自己的創作出現，也有了轟轟烈烈的光輝成就。然而，如同翻譯沉浸得過久的人一般，行文用字，不免有些「洋味」；這些劇本中，多多少少，便有西洋作品的影子存在。

舉例來說，胡適先生創作的劇本「終身大事」，劇中女主角田亞梅為了爭取婚姻自由而奮鬥，最後終於出走，顯然受到了易卜生筆下「傀儡家庭」（A Doll's House）的影響。

洪深與曹禺，是我國的名劇作家，然而，也因他們沉浸西洋劇作已久，以致成名作中，令人依稀有「似曾相識」的感受。洪深留學美國，他所寫的「趙閻王」；以及以「雷雨」聞名於世的曹禺，在「原野」一劇中，都有主角殺人及逃進森林，聽見鼓聲而產生幻覺，這兩個劇本的這一段，不約而同都脫胎於奧尼爾（Eugene O'nell）的「瓊斯皇帝」（Emperor Jones），西洋戲劇移人之深，由此可見一斑。

抗戰時期，從西方迻譯過來的劇本雖多，只不過都當成文學作品來欣賞；而當時我國舞臺劇盛極一時，創作名劇甚多，却很少聽說有人將這些劇本譯成外文，俾使全世界知道中國劇作家的功力與成就，這也是翻譯界的一個「盲點」。

政府自大陸播遷臺灣以來，將外國舞臺劇譯為中文，上演非常成功的不少，不說各大學戲劇系的期終演出，張道藩改編法國雨果（Hugo）的「狄四娘」（Angelo）；以及王錫茞、吳青萍合譯的偉大的薛巴斯坦」（The Great Sebastians），演出都曾轟動一時。

尤其，曾娶過絕世佳人瑪麗蓮夢露的美國劇作家亞瑟・米勒（Arthur Miller），一九四九年他所寫的「推銷員之死」（Death of a Salesman），雖然得過普立茲獎，以前在我國卻只為學校選讀作品之一，可是近年卻枯木逢春，海峽兩岸先後紛紛在「國家劇院」演出，聲勢之隆，超過了中國人自己編的舞臺劇多多，誠屬異數，也使人感慨良多。

王爾德的劇本，也備受國人歡迎，民國十三年，洪深把他的「少奶奶的扇子」譯為中文上演，極受歡迎。法國翻譯界有句名言說：「名著須二十年一譯。」想不到相隔近七十年之後，果然有人又在重譯斯劇，要以新的語言，來呈現這個劇本的新貌了。

我們不禁要問：為什麼沒有人將我國的舞臺劇本譯為外文，從西洋戲劇的陰影下走出來呢？如果從字源來闡釋，文字翻譯應該在舞臺劇施展不出半點兒力量，Drama這個字兒源於希臘文，意義為「做、作、演」（to do, act, perform），定義頗像現代的「默劇」與「舞劇」。可是到了後來，舞臺劇便多彩多姿起來，「牛津大字典」所下的定義為：採用散文或詩歌的文體，在舞臺上演出，依對話、動作的方式，佐之以現實生活中的姿態、衣着、與景致呈現，以敍述一個故事。

自從舞臺劇有了對話，翻譯的人，才能一盡所長，搭起溝通文化交流的橋樑。不過，除開熊式一譯的「王寶釧」與「西廂記」、楊世彭在美國譯導的「烏龍院」以後，中劇外譯的工作，雖然有人在默默耕耘，但却沒有得到應有的重視，更不必說社會與國家的支持了。

六

飛機失事以後

民國六十七年前後，現任國立成功大學文學院院長閻振瀛，他以留美的戲劇博士之身，先後翻譯了吳若的「天長地久」，姚一葦的「一口箱子」；和張永祥的「風雨故人來」，並且由東吳大學的學生，在「世界劇展」中演出，造成了一陣轟動，可是這些譯作，並沒有刊印成集，無法傳諸久遠，實在可惜。

然而，就在八十年十一月迄今，卻有兩本中文英譯舞臺劇本出版，使人振奮，「中劇外譯」，終於又跨出一大步了。

寫作劇本前後四十二年的姜龍昭，將他所寫作的二十四個舞臺劇中，挑選出「淚水的沉思」與「飛機失事以後」兩個劇本，由蔣娉女士譯成了英文。

劇本翻譯的重點在人物與對話。出場的角色該譯一個甚麼名字，看似無關宏旨，但其實這絕不是一個小問題。以姚克譯的「推銷員之死」來說，他譯 Willy Loman 為「惟利·羅門」，連名帶姓都譯，可是譯 Mildred Dunnock，卻又只譯「鄧諾克」這個姓了。他這種譯法可作文學作品來欣賞研讀，卻不宜於發揮原著的最大功能——搬上舞臺。如臺上中國的演員，卻說些洋調洋腔的話，觀眾怎麼能在不知不覺中入戲？所以劇本翻譯過不了這一關，譯出來儘管「忠實於原文」，卻只有廟堂裡供養的份兒。所以，阿瑟米勒授權海峽兩岸演出「推銷員之死」時，指定要用英若誠的譯本，這可能是很大的關鍵。

蔣娉譯「淚水的沈思」與「飛機失事以後」這兩個劇本，獨闢己見，她大踏步走出「對原著忠實

」的層次，而升高到「對讀者忠實」的境界。深知道劇本的功能就是要在舞臺上演，要演出成功，就先要能使臺上演員與臺下的觀眾打成一片，爲了不使英語觀眾，有下意識的排斥，她將劇本中的人名，一律「洋化」。

在「淚」劇中，她將主角莊秉剛譯爲Ben，邱素素譯爲Sue，莊執中逕譯爲John⋯⋯只有幾個配角：老吳、方董、姚經理，才譯爲Mr. Woo, Mr. Fong & Mr Yeh。這種人名翻譯，也有所本，霍克思譯「紅樓夢」，便是這個辦法。

而在「飛」劇中，更是洋化得徹底，桑炳成譯Ben，桑太太譯Sandy，他們的長子德正爲Ted，德昌爲Fay⋯⋯這些譯名，看似與原著脫節，其實卻是以負責的態度，使英語讀者在熟悉的人名稱呼中，從而領悟劇作的本旨。

蔣娉在人名迻譯上，並不是信手拈來，而是有過一番愼重的考慮，例如在「飛機失事以後」這個劇本中，有一個三花臉的角色：項必均，是個拉保險的業務員，一開始便登場，爲使觀眾進入趣味的境界。桑家的「下女」阿香接待他：

阿香：先生，你貴姓，找我們老爺，有什麼事嗎？

項：小姐（有些口吃，緊張）我⋯⋯姓項，項羽的項，名字叫必均⋯⋯

香⋯（訝異）甚麼？你叫『橡皮筋』⋯⋯

這小小幾句的插科打諢，會逗引讀者與觀眾一笑，但我卻沉思，英文該怎麼譯，才能貼切。看到

譯文，方始莞爾。

Shane: Sir, please have some tea. What is your name? You are here for Mr. Sand-

　　ers?

Robert: Yes, miss, my name is Robert Bond. I am here to……

Shane: What? Your name is Rubber band? Are you serious……?

蔣娉把項必成譯爲Robert Bond，這是英語世界中最熟悉的一個姓，電影中英國〇〇七情報員便是龐德啊，而又與「橡皮筋」rubber band諧音，眞使人拍案叫絕…「虧她想得出來！」

譯人名雖是小道，但要譯得妥貼，卻不容易，由此可以得到證明。

舞臺劇的對話翻譯，注定了劇本迻譯成敗的關鍵，蔣娉參與過電影工作，又擔任過電視節目的主持人，在美國主修美國文化研究，前後在美居留達二十四年之久，夫婿又是美國人，由她來擔綱，譯出這兩個劇本，對話的流暢，眞個是遊刃有餘，溜極了。如果不照着英譯本往下看，眞有點兒使人覺得，這原是她的一個英語劇本，只是由姜龍昭改譯成了中文，翻譯到了這種如影隨形，難分爾我，眞是接近「化境」了。

不過，各國語文中，自有其本身的文化特色，有些文句，尤其是成語，簡直就是無法照原文字句譯出。當然，如果把文學的「說故事」（Story telling）當成學術來研究，動輒加注，是一種流行的辦法；，然而這種辦法，要用在琅琅上口的舞臺劇，卻是一條走不通的死胡同。因此，這就要翻譯

者絞盡心血，才能尋出對等而恰巧的語句來表達了。

例如，在「淚」劇中，就有「狗咬呂洞賓，不識好人心」這一句臺詞，蔣娉無法向讀者與觀眾說明呂洞賓是何方神聖，就只有退而求其次，譯成平易近人的 People like that have no appreciation for anything，把這一句話的意思，同樣表達出來了。

此外，如「一是一、二是二」，她譯為 Straight forward．「六親不認」她譯為 Cold-hearted head-strong stubborn mule，也都是很適當的應變。

喜見「中劇外譯」，在我們等待了多年以後，終於又顯現了春天。蔣娉的翻譯，等於為國內的翻譯界注入了一股清流，如果他們賢伉儷，有志於譯，將來的成就必定不可限量。遠如英國譯托爾斯泰全集的米德夫婦，近如譯「紅樓夢」的楊憲益伉儷，都是斐聲世界譯壇的夫妻檔，希望姜龍昭的這兩個劇本，只是他們的啼聲初試，將來會有更多的譯品，呈現在國人之前。

黃文範　八一年五月四日

# 自 序

「飛機失事以後」這一個舞臺劇本，是我於民國八十年間十月完成的最新作品，想不到獲得蔣娉女士的讚賞，她以最快的速度，將之**翻譯**成了英文，成為我繼「淚水的沉思」後，出版的第二本中英文對照的劇本。

「淚水的沉思」中英文對照劇本出版後，荷蒙國防部總政戰部、僑委會、青年反共救國團等單位，大力支持，衷心銘感，尤其是行政院文建會購買了二百一十本，分贈本省各大專學校圖書館外，更寄送世界各大知名的圖書館蒐藏，使中國人寫的劇本，也有機會進入歐美、英、法、德、瑞等國家的知識寶庫，供人閱覽、研讀。

更令我興奮的是書寄出後，陸續收到國外圖書館寄來的道謝信，還有美國讀者要求購買該書的信函，更有德國的讀者，有意將之譯成德文，徵求我同意的函件，可見推動中西文學作品的交流，首要的關鍵，在多多出版中英對照的作品。

此外，國內著名的**翻譯**名家黃文範先生，對於蔣娉女士的迻譯手筆，靈活流暢，生動貼切，表示

十分讚賞，也是我願在此，特別提出向讀者報告，及向蔣女士表示感謝的。

「飛機失事以後」的故事，發生在民國八十年前後，本劇所要刻劃的，是臺灣經過經濟起飛，物質生活過度富裕以後，社會上所呈現的一些畸形怪現象。

年青的一代，好逸惡勞，追求刺激、吸毒、傳染愛滋病、綁票、強暴、勒索，無所不爲。年長的一輩，追逐金錢名利，進行走私、販毒的勾當、進口黑槍、春藥、毒品，牟取暴利，更進而製造僞善的假象、擾亂是非黑白的價值判斷。

「飛機失事以後」的主題，在強調善惡因果的報應，說明：「罪惡不是可以捐獻來洗刷乾淨的，名譽也不是可用金錢來購買裝飾的。」

人的善惡，也許可以欺矇世人於一時，但生命結束後，水落石出，眞相終有大白的一天。

我非常欣喜，本劇的出版，能獲得劇壇元老吳若先生，及翻譯名家黃文範先生所賜予的序文，更興奮的是蔣娉女士於譯畢全劇後，也給我寫了封信，她認爲這個劇本寫的比「淚水的沉思」，更爲成熟與嚴謹，因此，她翻譯的時候，也格外順手與流暢。她覺得全劇有精闢的哲學意味，字理行間更隱藏著很深厚的宗教意義與社會觀點，對於目前臺灣因經濟起飛，所引起的一些後遺症，有最好的闡述與印證。

劇中的對話、語氣、及稱謂：蔣娉說：她都採用美國的生活習慣用語，以免格格不入，基本上採用美國的戲劇技巧寫作方法。在人名的翻譯上，她很高興的在英文裡找到「項必均」這一人物的相似

名字，但劇中人取笑他口吃語氣的缺陷，則稍加約略刪改，因為，在國外從小就教育孩子，不可取笑有缺陷傷殘的人，當然壞人例外。

其次，她強調了桑母後悔沒有報警，將歹徒繩之以法的後果。至於第三幕第三場桑炳成死後靈魂復現，出場的部份，她只採用了旁白（O‧S）的手法，沒有用員人上場，如此，只是代表桑母的心理作用，可免於被人譏評為鬼魅神話。

蔣娉女士之翻譯本劇，從上面的說明中，可見她眞是化了不少的精神與心血。

為了讓大家，對蔣娉女士，多一點認識，我這裡簡單的，向大家作一番介紹。

她是中國人，祖籍江西九江，四川隆昌出生，在臺灣臺北長大，於一九六一年（民國五十年），在臺灣加入中央電影公司為基本演員，與影星王莫愁、丁強等合作拍攝過電影「蚵女」一片，及後又演出過劉碩夫導演的舞臺劇：「旋風」。民國五十一年十月臺灣電視公司開播，次年她與林璣、方靜靜、王戎合作演出「青春三鳳」劇集、與巴戈演出「溫暖人間」等電視劇，另外還擔任過電視節目「黃金時代」的主持人工作。

一九六四年她出任民航空運公司CAT空中小姐，一九六八年進入紐約派克學院（Packer Collegiate Institue）研究文學與戲劇，此一期間，她用心研讀了不少世界聞名的舞臺劇本。

一九七〇年進入美國紐澤西州瑞格士大學道格拉斯女子學院（Douglass College Rutgers University American Studies. B. A）繼續深造，主修美國文化研究，獲文學士學位。

迄一九九一年，前後在美居留了廿四年之久，因她的夫婿是美國人，所以她對中文，英文均有相當的造詣，本劇譯畢後，並特請夫婿John Sawyer Moxon予以過目校正，以求慎重。

我與蔣娉女士，相識於民國五十二年，那時我在臺灣電視公司任編審，並兼任製作「青春三鳳」節目。五十三年，她去了美國，就再也沒有聯絡，想不到民國七十九年，她回到臺北，才再度相見，相隔了廿多年，她對戲劇的狂熱，依舊不減當年，當民國八十年十月，臺北的「真善美劇團」演出我編寫的「一隻古瓶」舞臺劇時，她竟不計待遇，自費搭機專程返國，來參予該劇之演出，同時，也帶來了「淚水的沉思」的譯本，當時，我的「飛機失事以後」劇本，尚未完全脫稿，排戲之餘，我與她談及，她就一再敦促我早日完稿，……可以說，她是本劇的催生婆。

如今，我真不知怎麼說，才能表達我內心對她的感激。希望，在未來的歲月中，我們能再繼續合作下去。

這一次的封面圖樣，由中國電視公司的美術組長邱則明先生與美術設計師楊紀迪小姐共同為我精心設計。這一次的色彩，較諸「淚水的沉思」，更為鮮明突出，容易吸引讀者來閱覽，容我在此向他倆致誠摯的感謝。

最後，我衷心盼望，本劇能有機會，在國內外的舞臺上，早日以中文或英文演出，唯希望劇團演出前，能尊重著作權，先函臺灣臺北市八德路三段十二巷五十七弄十九號四樓，或電話：（〇二）七一五八二〇號徵求本人之同意許可。演出時，更希望註明編劇及譯者姓名，勿任意改動對白及情節

，若公開售票作營業性之演出，盼能酌付作者演出版權費，若有意改編為電影、電視或廣播劇，要事先徵求作者之同意。

姜龍昭　寫於民國八十一年五月十日

蔣娉與作者合影

# 「飛機失事以後」

（三幕舞臺劇）

時間：現代——民國七十九年或任何一年也可。

第一幕：九月間的某一天下午。

第二幕：距第一幕數天後。

第三幕：第一場十月間的某一天。

第二場相隔一星期後。

第三場相隔五天後。

地點：臺北市，或任何一城市也可。

佈景：三幕同一佈景，桑家客廳。

用象徵方式或寫實方式佈景均可。是一富有人家的豪華客廳，有樓梯可通樓上房間。客廳內，有一門通外面大門，另外有門通廚房、飯廳、及德昌、德正、德芬三人之臥室。客廳旁有一書房，內有小型保險箱、寫字桌、及沙發等物，書房內情形，觀眾可以看得見，有燈可開關。

客廳內有大小沙發、電視機、電話等設備，牆上有字畫、及「樂善好施」之匾額。另有一搖椅更佳。

第三幕，飛機失事以後，客廳內佈置一靈堂，牆上掛桑炳成遺像，橫几上有貢品及香燭臺等設物。

通大門口處，要有衣架、鞋櫃之玄關，方便掛衣物，屋內有豪華之玻璃吊燈，較有氣派，正中有長落地窗，可見院中花木，及天色之光線變化。牆上可有大型月曆或壁鐘，唯需注意與劇情進展相配合。

人物：：

桑炳成——五十餘歲，某貿易公司董事長，戴金絲眼鏡，略肥胖，精明能幹，商場高手。

桑太太——五十餘歲，面圓團富婆型，裝扮樸素，面容慈祥。

桑德正——廿五歲，大學末畢業即做事，花花公子，浮而不實。

桑德昌——十七歲尚在高中讀書，不學好，染上吸毒惡習。

桑德芬——炳成長女，十九歲，大學一年級生，純潔可愛，後因被綁票受辱，精神崩潰失常。

桑大成——炳成之姪子，廿八、九歲，在美國協助桑炳成經營商業。

馬淑貞——炳成的表妹，四十餘歲中年婦女，打扮較摩登，能言善道。

梁院長——愛愛孤兒院的院長，五十餘歲，帶黑框眼鏡。

二

劇情大概：

桑炳成是一家貿易公司的董事長，樂善好施，喜愛做善事，人皆目之為難得的好人，生有二子一女，長子德正在其公司上班，但並不認真工作，喜歡拈花惹草，頗為風流，次子在高中就讀也不學好，不幸染上吸毒惡習，難以戒絕。唯一愛女德芬，在大學就讀，清純可喜，不幸某次放學為歹徒綁架強暴，乃致精神失常，常想自殺，以求解脫。

桑炳成某次去泰國，有意投資做生意，孰知歸途中，在機場因機件發生故障，而空難喪亡。炳成死後，其妻發現了不少其夫生前的秘密，善惡因果之報應，真是令人難以相信。

項必成——人人保險公司的業務員，說話有些口吃，喜感人物。

老　黃——炳成家的司機，約四十餘歲，忠誠老實。

阿　香——桑家年輕的女佣人，約廿多歲，青春可喜。

# 第一幕

時：一個秋天的下午。

景：桑家客廳。

人：桑炳成、桑太太、桑德正、桑德昌、桑德芬、阿香、桑大成、項必均、梁院長、馬淑貞。

幕啓時：

阿香在收拾客廳，先是掃地，繼而擦拭傢具。

稍頃，門鈴響，她停止工作，出去開門。在大門外，引領了一個年青人項必均上。

項初入這一有錢人家的客廳，有些好奇的東張西望著。阿香去倒了一杯茶給他。

香：先生，……你貴姓，找我們老爺，有什麼事嗎？

項：小姐，（有些口吃，緊張時，咭咭吧吧，以產生笑的舞臺效果）我……姓項，……項羽的項，……

……名字叫必均，……

香：（訝異）什麼？你叫「橡皮筋」！……好有趣的名字！

項：我不是「橡……橡……皮筋」，我……是項……必……均，（取出一張名片）這……

是……我的名片。

香：（接過名片）喔，……項先生，……是必均，……不是皮筋……你找我們老爺……有什麼事嗎？

四

項：……「人人保險公司」的業務員，……！我是想……請你們老爺，……參加人壽保險，……定產業保險，……參加保險，有……有……很多……很多……好處！……

香：……好處？……全都是「騙」人的！……

項：（正色的）小姐，……你……你……你

香：我怎麼？

項：你……怎麼可以這麼說呢？我們是完全……為社會……大眾服務的……

香：說得是很好聽的，……過去我曾為我媽保了險，……結果，我媽死了，……去領保險費，……他們……就是不肯給，……說我媽早就有心臟病，……事先沒有什麼「告知」，……死了，……就是不能付保險費，……連已經繳的錢，也不退回！……害我爸，……差一點給氣死！……

項：小姐，……我們的「保險公司」，……可不一樣啊！……是和美國人……合作的，……死了，……絕……絕……。

香：你別絕了，……再絕……也是「不付錢」！……

項：（急了）小姐，……你……你……聽……聽……我說！……你看！……看，……我……像

項：壞人」嗎？……像「騙子」嗎？

香：（向之端詳了一番）……

項‧怎麼樣？……

香‧你臉上，雖沒有寫「壞」字，也沒有寫「好」字，……你呀，……還是請回吧！……我不會贊成

，老爺參加什麼「保險」的！……

項‧小姐，你……你……別趕我……見了你們……老爺，我……自然……會走的！（賴著不走）

香‧早說，……你是來拉保險的，……我就不開門，讓你進來了！……我看你，不是「橡皮筋」，……

……是「橡皮糖」！……黏住了，甩也甩不掉……

項‧小姐，……我是「項必均」，不是「橡皮糖」！……

（這時，桑太太自樓上走下來，進入客廳，邊走邊說）

母‧阿香，……你是跟誰在說話，……把我吵醒了！……

香‧太太，……是個拉保險的，他叫「橡皮筋」！……

項‧（上前）太太，……我不是「橡皮筋」，……我是「項……必均」，……這是我的名片。

母‧（已面對項，接過名片，看了一下）啊，……項先生，……對不起，我先生已經保過很多險了，

……你……請便吧！……

項‧太太，……我……是……第一次……來工作，……我……不會……說話，……這兒……（打開皮包取

出一些宣傳資料）有一些資料，可以留下來，……給你們參考，……若是……需要保險，……可

以打電話給我！……

母：也好！（接過資料）……我會給我先生看的！……你可以走了！……

項：謝謝，……（走了出去，快到門口時，又折回）別忘了，打電話給我，……我叫項必均！……

香：知道了，……項先生，請吧！

（項走出，阿香重重將門關上）

母：阿香，……以後，有客人來，先問清楚了，……再讓他進來，……現在社會上，壞人很多，……非處處小心不可。

香：是，太太。……

（德芬穿了件漂亮的衣服，手裡拿了幾本書，自她的臥室走出）

芬：媽，……你看！（在母面前轉了一個圈）我穿的這件衣服，漂不漂亮？……

母：（讚賞地）漂亮！……德芬，……你真是越長越漂亮了！

芬：是不是跟媽媽年輕時候一模一樣了！……

母：瞧你，……真會拍媽的馬屁，……今兒，星期六，下午學校裡還有課嗎？

芬：有呀！「社會學」，……還是必修課呢！

母：好好唸，……等你大學畢業了，……媽還想送你出國去留學呢！

芬：真的嗎？

母：媽幾時騙過你？……德芬，……你哥哥和你小弟，……都不是讀書的料，……唉，……談起他們兩個，真讓媽傷心。

芬：媽，……大哥雖說大學沒讀完，……現在，……在爸的公司裡，不也做的好好的嗎？……

母：那是因為他是你爸的兒子，……換了別人，也許早就把他開除了，……三天兩頭，在辦公室找不到他的人，總是和一些不三不四的朋友，在外面喝酒玩女人，……將來，我真不知道，他怎麼能繼承他父親的事業。……

芬：媽，……你該要爸爸，好好管教他才行！……

母：你爸整天忙得什麼似的，……那兒有時間管教他！……

芬：媽，……我最近在學校裡參加了一個「博愛社」的社團，下個月打算去山地鄉，為一些貧苦的山胞，做一些服務的工作，現在正在籌募經費，希望大家踴躍捐獻，……媽，……我想多捐一點，你說好不好？

母：德芬，……你想捐多少？

芬：（商量的口吻）媽，……我想捐十萬！……好不好？

母：德芬，別人捐多少？……你比別人多一點，不就行了，……何必這麼招搖！

芬：媽，……捐十萬也不算多嗎！……何必這樣小氣，……你看，……爸每一次支持什麼慈善活動，義賣義演的，一出手，不是五十萬，就是一百萬的！……

母：好了，……別說了，媽依你，……十萬就十萬，只要是做「好事」，媽絕對支持你，……只是，你現在讀大學，讀書還是最要緊，別老是參加什麼課外活動，……現在有些大學生，一會兒示威遊行，一會兒又是絕食抗議，……真是太不像話！……德芬，……你不會這樣子吧！

芬：媽，……你放心，……那些政治活動，……我才沒有興趣去參加呢！

母：這……才是我的乖女兒。……

（這時桑父穿着襯衫，未着上裝，邊打領帶，邊自樓梯上走下來）

母：炳成，……還早呢！……為什麼不多睡一會兒！……

父：愛愛孤兒院的梁院長，快來了，（看了看手錶）……我總不能等她來了，……我才起床呀！……

德芬，……來，……讓爸爸，好好看看你。……

芬：爸，……我好久都沒看見你了，……瞧你，……忙得好像瘦多了！……

父：是嗎？……（母這時悄悄走上樓去）

芬：爸，……還是保重身體要緊！……別只顧着賺錢，把什麼都忘了！……爸，……你說對不對？

父：（微笑）對，……真想不到我的女兒，一眨眼，……都懂得這麼多了！……聖經上說：「你若是賺得了全世界，却賠上了自己的生命，又有什麼益處呢！」……爸，……你說對不對？

芬：爸，……你還這麼小的時候，……老要爸抱着，上街買「熱狗」給你吃的事嗎？……現在，……都是「大學生」了，……時間過得真快呀！……

九

芬：爸，……你答應過我，……到我廿歲生日的時候，……要給我開一個盛大的生日舞會，好好的給我慶祝一番，……你沒忘記吧？

父：這麼重要的一件大事，……我怎麼會忘記呢？……我還答應，到你生日的那一天，我要送你一個鑽戒，作為送你的「生日禮物」，……將來，……等你結婚的時候，……可以作為交換飾物之用。……

芬：爸，……我還年輕，……什麼「結婚」，……還遙遠得很呢？

父：（正色的）告訴爸，……現在，有要好的男朋友了沒有？要是有的話，……把他帶回家來，……先讓老爸看一下啊！

芬：爸，……我還沒有男朋友，……要是有一天，有了，……我一定把他先帶回來，……通過「老爸」這一關！

父：你可要說話算話啊！……

（這時，母已拿了一件父的西裝上衣，自樓上下來）

母：秋天了，……快穿上吧，……別受了涼，又鼻子不通了。……

（母為父穿上上衣）

芬：（看看手錶）媽，……我得到學校上課去了，……你答應給我捐的十萬塊錢，什麼時候給我？……

……

一〇

母：明天吧，……我現在手邊沒有這麼多！

父：什麼十萬塊錢？

母：是德芬學校裡，一個社團在籌募經費，希望大家捐獻，……德芬要我多捐一點，……我答應她的

父：什麼社團哪？……

芬：是個慈善社團，專門做社會福利工作的！……

父：既然是慈善事業，……十萬太少了，……爸，……現在就開支票給你帶去！……好不好？……

芬：（高興的送上老爸一吻）爸，……太好了！……你……真是我的好爸爸！

（父取出支票簿寫好數字，蓋上圖章，撕下給芬）

母：德芬，……放了學，早點回家，別在外面亂逛，……現在社會治安很不好，坐計程車，要找個伴，知道嗎？……昨兒，晚上，阿香出去買東西，……就遇上了個「色狼」，……嚇得她逃回來，臉都發白了！……

芬：媽，……我上學去了！……

父：（叮囑）德芬，……我自己會小心的！……

芬：媽，……別太大意了，……現在歹徒太多了，真要是有人把你綁票了，或是強暴了，

二一

芬：爸，……我和你媽，……都會急死的，知道嗎？……

　　　我又不是小孩子，……我會照顧自己的，……ＢＹＥ，ＢＹＥ，……

　　（芬說完輕鬆的開門走出去）

父：太太，……兩個兒子呢？……有沒有在家？……

母：大的出去了，說是一個老同學，最近從國外回來，……在一家餐廳聚餐，……大概，一會兒就回來了吧！

父：小的呢？……學校不是寄通知書來，……說他老是「缺課」，這是怎麼回事？你也不注意看著他一點！

母：腳在他身上，……我怎麼看得住，……我去看看，也許他在房裡睡大覺！

　　（母說著去開德昌臥室的門，進入，不久即出）

父：怎麼？不在？……

母：八成，又去打電動玩具去了，……這孩子，……是着了迷了！……跟他說了多少遍了！……沒有用，……就像往牆上刷「白粉」一樣！……

父：（嘆息）唉，……難怪大家喜歡開電動玩具店，……錢好賺嚜！……

　　（門鈴響，阿香出，去開門，不久引梁院長自外進入客廳）

香：太太，……是梁院長來了。……

母：噢，……（阿香去倒茶）梁院長，請坐，……我先生，……知道你要來，……已等了一陣了！

父：（自口袋取出一張事先已寫好的支票，交給梁）梁院長，……這是一張即期支票，……你去銀行，馬上就可以領到現款的！

梁：（接過支票一看，驚訝地）啊，……壹百萬，……桑董事長，你捐給我們「愛愛孤兒院」壹百萬？……

父：梁院長，……你爲「愛愛孤兒院」奉獻了一生，……我桑炳成，捐壹百萬，也是應該的，……你收養的孩子這麼多，每個月的開銷又這麼大，……現在物價又在飛漲，捐十萬、廿萬，是派不上什麼用處的！……

梁：桑董事長，……我代表院裡一百多個孩子，向你致謝，……這些年來，……你經常是我們院裡最大的經濟支柱，……我眞不知該說什麼，才能表達我對你的感激！……

父：梁院長，不必客氣，……「爲善最樂」，……做好事，是每一個人的責任。……不是嗎？

梁：桑董事長，……做好事，是有好報的，……所謂：「善有善報，惡有惡報」，……你這樣熱心的做好事，……將來，一定會有好的結果的！……我現在，……就把收據開給你，……（說著打開皮包來，寫收據）

父：梁院長，不忙吧！……今後，院裡若有什麼特別的需要，可以隨時來找我，……只要我能辦到的

一三

，……我一定儘量來配合！

母：梁院長，……我先生，有事忙，不空的話，……你打電話給我也是一樣，……只要是慈善事業，……我們絕對是支持的！

（梁將收據寫好，交父）

梁：桑董事長，這收據請你收下，……希望董事長有空的話，……到我們院裡來參觀，……董事長夫人，……也一起來。……

父：好，……有空的時候，……我和我太太，……一定會帶些糖果，去看看孩子們！

梁：董事長，……那我告辭了。……

父：梁院長，……要不要我叫司機老黃，開車送你回去？……

梁：不用了，……謝謝董事長，董事長夫人，……再見。（出門下）

父：（送至門口）再見。

（電話響，母接聽）

母：喂，……你是大成？……什麼？……你現在在桃園機場，……你從美國回來了！……好，……我叫他來聽電話！

（母交話筒給父）

母：是大成打來的電話！

父：我是二叔啊！……好！……我在家等你，……你趕快來，……一切，見了面詳談。……（掛上電話）

母：炳成，……你要大成在美國，給你進口什麼貨物，……神秘兮兮地，……問你，還不肯說。……

父：（不耐煩地）太太，放心，不是「女人」就是了！……你看，我像是個做不法買賣的生意人嗎？……

母：你越是這樣說，……我越是想知道，……究竟進口的是什麼「東西」？……

父：好吧，我告訴你，……是一些「古董」，……我們中國的「古董」，……有瓷器的花瓶，也有銅器的鼎呀什麼的！……可以賺不少錢喔！

母：貿易公司的事，我一向都不過問的嗎？……

父：你這麼說清楚了，……我就放心了！

母：（看看錶）太太，……我現在到公司去一下，……等下晚上回來吃飯，大成來的話，……要他別走，……去準備些菜，我要和他喝兩杯。

母：好，……我知道了。

父：阿香，……叫老黃把車開出來，……我現在要到公司去。

香：老爺，……老黃早就把車開出來了！……他在等你呢！……

（父自衣架上拿了，戴上出去）

母：阿香，……去廚房看看，……要廚子老劉，多準備幾個菜，姪少爺，……等下來吃晚飯。……

香：是，太太。（向廚房下）

母：奇怪，……都三點多了，德正、德昌一個也不回來，不會出了什麼事吧？……

（門鈴響）

母：大概是德正回來了，……阿香，快去開門。

（阿香應聲自內出，去開門，自外面引進來，一個打扮得很時髦的中年女人，嗓門響亮的叫著）

馬：表嫂，……表哥，他在家嗎？

母：阿香，快去倒茶。……

馬：我不喝茶，……我要來杯摩卡咖啡。……（阿香去沖咖啡下）

母：淑貞，……好久不見了，……這一陣子，你到那兒去啦！

馬：我啊，……才從東南亞旅遊回來，……眞累極了！……看來看去，……還是在臺灣最好。表嫂，……你怎麼不和表哥一起出國去玩玩呢！……

母：我……懶得很，……你表哥啊，……忙着做貿易生意，也走不開！……對了，淑貞，今兒，是什麼風把你吹來了，……眞是好久沒見你來找我聊天了。

馬：表嫂，……我是無事不登三寶殿，今兒是特地來求表哥，看能不能幫我一個忙。

母：他呀，……到公司去了，……有什麼事？你跟我說也一樣，只要能辦到的，我們一定幫忙。

（阿香送上二杯咖啡後，退下）

馬：（喝了一口咖啡後，才開始說）事情是這樣的，我有個親戚，最近，和大陸上的朋友做生意，運

來一大批中藥。……想不到，到了臺灣，貨在船上，被海關查到，扣留了下來。……

母：是不是「走私」運進來的？

馬：是託漁船幫忙運的，……那批中藥，都是很名貴的藥材，有人參、鹿茸，……至少值到五、六百

萬呢？

母：喔，……值不少錢吶！

馬！是呀，……若是給沒收了，多可惜。他們想，請我表哥，是不是可以託個熟人，找海關的主官去

說個情，……罰點錢算了，貨還是發還給他們，不要充公。

母：（為難也）這……

馬：表嫂，……若是需要送「紅包」，去打通關節，他們也願意！

母：淑貞，這件事，我清楚，炳成，他是不會答應的。

馬：表嫂，……表哥不是最願意幫人忙，做好事的嗎？……怎麼不會肯幫忙呢？

母：他啊，凡是慈善事業找他捐獻或是義賣，他是絕對不會打退票的，……要他去關說，託人情，…

…他是最不肯合作的，尤其是走私、非法買賣，他一向是不願介入的，……他常在我面前說

，……做人，一定要做得正，……這樣，在社會上，才能受人尊敬，被人看得起。

馬：表嫂，……你說得很對，……表哥這樣也沒有錯，只是我那親戚說，他那批貨，若是真的被沒收

充公，……他活不下去，就只好去跳海自殺了。……

母：是嗎？……有這麼嚴重嗎？

馬：若不是這麼嚴重，表嫂，我也不會專程來找表哥幫忙，……我那親戚說，……那筆貨的資本，……一大部份，還是借了高利貸來湊成的！……表嫂，所謂「救人一命，勝造七級浮屠」……你不也最熱心做好事的嗎？……這可真是做好事啊！

母：淑貞，……不是我不想做好事，……實在是你不清楚你表哥的性格。他呀，你要他捐錢，做好事，那絕沒問題，你要他去「送紅包」、「講人情」，就是他自己的事，都不會去做，何況是代人去說。在公司裡，還有一些公開場合裡，他常說：「做人，人格最重要；做事，要走正路，這樣上，……才能受人尊重，被人看得起。」……你想請他幫這個忙，恐怕，……很難！……

馬：表嫂，你是他太太，……就算是你的親戚，也不成嗎？

母：過去，我已碰過好幾次釘子了，……他的固執，……誰也拿他沒有辦法！……若是你不死心，當面去求他，試試看，也好，……說真的，海關方面，他確是認識不少朋友，……再說，你親戚走私運進來的，只是一些中藥，又不是什麼嗎啡、海洛因毒品，害人的東西，看在你是她表妹的份上，……也許他會答應，也說不定。

馬：他人，現在公司嗎？

母：一會兒，就回來了，……他說要回來吃晚飯的，淑貞，……你也不忙走，……就在這兒等他，……

…在我們家吃便飯！

馬：可是，人家急得像熱鍋上的螞蟻一樣，……急著等我的回音哪！

母：好吧！……我現在打電話去，催他趕緊回來。……（急忙撥電話）喂，……丁秘書嗎？……我是董事長太太，……請問我先生，是不是還在公司辦公？……什麼？……他已經走了，……回家來了！……好，……沒事了，謝謝你，丁秘書，再見。……（掛上電話）好了，……你也甭急了，……他一會兒，就回來了！……

馬：那，……我就不走了！……

母：淑貞，……是不那批貨的「資金」裡面，你也有一份，……所以，才這麼著急？……對不對！……

……

馬：要不是我也有「份」，……才懶得來管這些閒事吶！……

（門鈴響，阿香去開門）

母：也許，正是他回來了。

（阿香引大少爺德正自外上，德正頭上包了紗布，左手吊了個繃帶，掛在胸前，母見其狼狽相，嚇了一大跳）

馬：德正，……你怎麼啦？……誰把你打成這樣？……你不是說，……去參加同學會聚餐的嗎？……

母：德正，……你……要不要緊？……怎麼會這樣呢？……是發生了車禍？……

正：媽，姑媽，……別緊張，……我只是受了些皮肉之傷，……我已經去看過了醫生，……醫生說，休養幾天，……就可以復原的。

母：你的手，是怎麼啦？……是和人打架，對不對？

馬：德正，究竟是發生了什麼事？……你快說呀！

正：起先，……我是和幾個老同學，在一個餐廳聚餐，吃飯的時候，喝了點酒，後來，我們一起去卡拉ＯＫ玩，……誰知道，……碰上了幾個流氓，……結果，一言不合，就幹了起來，……玻璃杯、麥克風就遭了殃，……嘿，……後來，他們中間，有人開了一鎗，……警察聞聲追來，……才逃走了。

母：聽你這麼說，……真把我嚇壞了，德正，……要是開的那一鎗，打中了你，……你還能活命嗎？

正：媽，……他才沒有這個「種」呢！……你放心，……他只是拿鎗來唬人的！……

馬：德正，……以後，……這種危險的地方，……你還是少去，……免得你媽為你就心！……

正：姑媽，……你放心，……我又不是小孩子了，……這種場面，……我見得多了，……

母：德正，……媽現在鄭重的警告你，……以後，……你再隨便和人在外面打架鬧事，……你就不要再回這個家！

正：（辯說）媽，你不知道，現在社會上，是吃硬不吃軟的，……你越軟弱，別人就越欺侮你，……

你越兇越狠，別人就怕你，……不敢來碰你，惹你！……

（門鈴響，汽車喇叭聲，阿香去開門，不久引父入，父脫帽）

馬：表哥，……你回來了？

母：淑貞，……等了你很久了。……

（德正見父進入，急躲入自己的臥室去，但已被父看見）

父：淑貞，……你來找我，……準是有什麼事？……沒事，你是不會來的！……（坐下沙發，阿香送上一隻專用的保溫杯）

馬：表哥，……是這樣的，……我有個親戚，最近和大陸上的朋友，做生意運來一批中藥，結果貨在船上，被海關查到，扣留了下來，……表哥在海關的熟人，不是很多嗎？……是不是可以去說個人情，罰點錢「了」事，……貨還是發還給他們，不要充公。……

父：是走私進來的，對不對？

馬：是啊！……

父：表妹，……最近，……這樣的事，太多了，……對不起，……我……愛莫能助，……你……另請高明吧！……

馬：表哥，……這批貨，要值好幾百萬，……我也是其中股東一份子，……能不能看在我的份上，幫一個忙，……就是要送「紅包」，……我們也願意！……

二一

父：表妹，……別的忙，我可以幫，……這件事，……恕我無能為力。……

馬：（用軟功）表哥，……你真忍心「見死不救」嗎？……

父：（嘆氣）表妹，……你怎麼，……這樣說呢？……你要知道，我在社會上，是有聲望的人，……若是我答應你，幫你這個忙，……將來傳了出去，……我的「形象」，就被徹底破壞了，……說得「白」一點，我就沒法「混」了，你知道嗎？……

馬：（知已絕望）好了，表哥，……你別說了，我走了。……

母：淑貞，你不吃了飯，再走嗎？……

馬：我……怎麼還吃得下飯！……

父：淑貞，……你損失多少錢，……告訴我，……我可以補償你。……

馬：不用了，……表哥，……你自己留著用吧，……我走了。

（馬生氣地，逕自開門離去）

父：這是沒有辦法的事！……

母：炳成，……你看，……你把表妹得罪了。

父：（嘆息）唔……

母：（突想起）咦，德正呢？……剛才，我看見他頭上包著紗布，……手上吊了綳帶，是不又和人打架了？……

母：嗯！……不過，……還好，醫生說只是皮肉之傷，休養一兩天，就可以復原的！

父：叫他出來，我有話和他說。

母：（走向德正的臥室，在門外叫）德正，……你出來一下，……爸……有話和你說。

（德正膽怯地自臥室走出來）

正：爸──，……

父：你的傷，……真是皮肉之傷嗎？……

正：醫生是這麼說的！……休養一兩天，就會好的！……

父：那後天可以上班嗎？

正：我想……可以的。

父：（正色的）德正，……你今年廿五歲了，……應該算是成年人了，……怎麼還是像那些沒長大的青少年一樣呢？……爸像你這樣年紀的時候，也已經開始在社會上做事了。……你大學讀了一年，不想讀了，我也不勉強你……讓你在公司上班，……你就該好好的多虛心學習，……我……辛辛苦苦掙來的這些產業，……將來，還不是由你來接棒。……

正：爸，你別說了，這些我都知道。……

父：這些日子，你在公司不好好的上班不說，還在外面喝酒、打牌、玩女人，你別以為我不知道，我隨時派人在暗中注意你的行動。……這就是考核，你知道嗎？……

二三

正：爸，……我慢慢改進就是了。

父：我跟你說，下個月，我要去一趟泰國，可能要一個月才回來。……

母：你去泰國，作什麼？

父：自然是去談做生意的事情，我打算在那邊，建立一兩個據點。……順便，也去看幾個老朋友。

正：爸，……我想跟你一起去。

父：暫時不必了。我打算去以前，先要總經理升你做業務部經理，……看你能不能挑得動這付擔子。若是你行，那我也沒辦法，只好把公司這份事業，交給別人來管理，你聽清楚了沒有？

正：聽清楚了。

父：做了經理，我特別交付你一個任務，希望你能達成！

正：什麼任務？

母：炳成，你們談，我去廚房，看一下。

父：好，你去忙你的。

（母向廚房下）

父：我要你暗中調查，對公司的各級主管，包括總經理、副總經理在內，等我回來的時候，給我一份詳細的書面考核資料。包括他們的工作能力、勤惰、私生活，以及他們對公司的向心力，你能辦

二四

正：爸，……我認真去做，就是了。

正：我一方面要你考核別人，另一方面，我也要別人，在暗中考核你，同樣的，他們也會給我一份，對你的考核資料。……

父：我一方面要你考核別人，另一方面，我也要別人，在暗中考核你，同樣的，他們也會給我一份，對你的考核資料。……

正：爸……你好厲害。

父：德正，我告訴你，……要做一個成功的總經理，必先要能做好「認人」這件工作。……認識一個人，不是簡單的一件事。因為人會偽裝，做假。表面和實際，往往並不相符。壞人的臉上，往往寫的是個「好」字。有些「偽」君子，戴上了面具，跟真君子沒有兩樣。德正，大家都說……「做人難」，換一個角度，我認為「認人，比做人更難」，……現在，你才起步，……別忘了，爸給你說的這些話！

正：爸，……我會記得。……

（門鈴響，阿香去開門，旋即引大成自外上）

香：老爺，……侄少爺來了。

成：二叔，……德正，你怎麼啦？……

正：不要緊的，大成哥，……你……剛從美國來？……

成：嗯！

父：德正，……你下去吧，……

正：是。（走向自己臥室下）

父：大成，……你辛苦了。

成：還好，……因為塞車，……來遲了一回兒。

父：沒有關係，……來，……到……我書房裡去談。

成：好。

（父領大成，進入書房，打開電燈，坐下，大成打開皮包拿出一些文件，給父看，二人竊竊私語，談一些生意上的事，觀眾聽不見。）

（母自內出，阿香泡二杯茶，送入書房後，退出）

母：阿香，侄少爺來了？（打開客廳的燈）

香：嗯。

母：要廚房把碗筷擺好，……準備開飯。

香：是，太太。（入廚房下）

（這時德昌背了書包，悄悄自外推門而入）

母：德昌，……你怎麼晚，才回來。……

昌：（看見書房燈亮，膽怯地問）媽，……爸回來啦？……

母：嗯！……快去洗個臉，把書包放下，……準備吃飯啦！……

昌：媽，……你再給我一點錢，好不好？……吃完飯，我和同學要去買參考書！

母：多少？

昌：五千。

母：……

昌：五千。

母：怎麼？昨天給你的錢，全花光啦！……

昌：我去電動玩具店，玩「柏青哥」，……手氣不好，輸了嗎！……

母：年紀這麼小，……就學會了賭博！……是老師教的嗎？

昌：（調皮的）老師沒有教，……是同學教的！……（再伸手）

母：唔，……（把五千塊錢給昌）慢慢用，知道嗎？……

昌：（數錢）一、二、三、四、五。媽，……你真好。……（放入口袋）

母：快去洗臉去。

昌：是，媽。（進入洗手間去，下）

母：炳成，……（走向書房）是不可以開飯了？

父：好，……馬上開飯。……

（父與成收拾好東西，走出書房）

二七

父：大成，……為了慶祝這一次生意成功，……我們好好乾兩杯。

成：謝謝二叔。……對了，二叔，……這一次回來，……我帶了瓶法國香水，送給你，……（自皮箱內取出一瓶香水給母）你打開聞聞看，香不香？

母：（打開香水聞一下）嗯，真香，……大成，……你一路辛苦了，……我們先吃飯吧，……邊吃邊談。……

成：是，二嬸。……

（眾人正欲進入飯廳，忽電話鈴響，阿香接聽後，說）

香：老爺，找你的電話。

父：（去接聽）喂，……我就是桑炳成。……你說什麼？……

（父神色不對，眾人也注意傾聽，這時透過麥克風，播出電話中陌生人的聲音說：「桑董事長，你的女兒德芬，現在在我們的手裡，……希望你馬上準備五千萬現鈔，……於三天內贖回，……否則有生命之危險，……聽清楚了沒有？……最後，警告你，不准報警，……否則，……你走著瞧！……」（電話掛斷）

父：喂，……喂，……怎麼？還沒說清楚，就掛斷了呢？

成：二叔，……德芬，給綁票了？

父：忍，……也們要五千萬，……還不佳報警。

昌：五千萬？

（德正、德昌各自臥室走出）

正：爸，……怎麼啦？……誰被綁票了？……

昌：是姐姐嗎？……媽……？……

父：（沉着的）太狠了，……一開口，……就是五千萬？……

（燈暗）

——幕徐徐下。

# 第二幕

時：距第一幕數天後

景：桑家客廳

人：桑炳成、桑太太、桑德正、桑德昌、桑德芬、阿香、老黃、桑大成、項必均、梁院長、馬淑貞

幕啓時：

德正已解除了手上吊的繃帶，頭上的紗布仍在，他在看著報紙。炳成則坐在電話機旁的沙發上，猛抽香煙，一口接一口，二人均不說話，空氣十分沉悶。

父：……喂。……我就是炳成，……怎麼？……你在那兒，已經等了一個多小時了，……沒見有人來會面，……會不會又改地點了！……別……急著走，……也許，再等一回，……會面的人，就出現了。……（掛上電話）

正：爸，是媽打來的電話？

父：嗯！……已經換了好幾個地方了！……就是不見他們的人露面，……這不是明明在拿人開心嗎！

正：爸，……別管他，……我們，還是去報警，算了！……這些綁匪，實在太可惡了，……非把他們抓起來，繩之於法不可，……否則社會永遠不能安寧。……

父：德正，事情不會像你說得那樣簡單。報了警，萬一抓不到他們，那我們不就慘了，……碰上這種事，……我們還是認作「破財消災」算了。

正：爸，……這不是辦法！……你這樣怕他們，……這樣，他們吃到了甜頭，說不定，綁了這一次，還會再來綁第二次。……

父：怎麼？……你想和我「抬槓」？……

正：這不是「抬槓」，……爸，……我們偷偷去報警，……歹徒怎麼會知道呢？……報了警，……至少還有把他們抓到的機會，……現在這樣，白白送錢去，不等於肉包子打狗嗎？……（思索了一下）不，我決定……還是去「報警」！……（起立欲外出，父急起立將之拖住！）

父：（喝止）你去報警，……萬一，……他們一狠心，……把妳妹妹，……強暴、或是撕了票，……

你再後悔也來不及了！……

正：（只好屈服）好，……我不報警！……

（這時，突然門鈴響）

父：會不會……是你媽回來了？……

正：不會……是你媽回來了？

正：不像！……

父：那會是誰呢？……阿香，……去開門。

正：爸，……他說，是來找你的！他姓項……

正：（狐疑的）項……先生，……我可不認識你呀！……

（德正外出開門，不久引進來的是項必均，那個拉保險的！……）

正：阿香出去買菜了，……我去開門。

項：（取出名片遞上）桑董事長，……這是我的名片，……我叫項必均（依然口吃），……是「人人

保險公司」的業務員，……我來找你好幾次了，……你都不在家，……今天，……真……是……巧…

…巧……極了。

父：項先生，……你找我有什麼貴幹？……是……希望……我參加保險，是不是？……

項：（喜極）對……對……極了，……保……保險……有很多……很多的……好處！……譬如說…「

三一

天……天有……不測……測風雲，……人……人……有……

項……對……對……極了，……桑……董事長，……對……不起，……我……一急，……就會……口……

正……（看他咭咭巴巴，索性接上）旦夕禍福！……

項……對，……是絕……絕不會錯的！……

父……（很好笑）我……覺得貴公司，會派你這樣的人才，……來拉保險，……真是一絕！……

……吃，……你要……多……多……原諒。……

父……好了，……長話短說，……你想要我投保多少，……你自己說，正好，……下個月，我要去大陸探親，……你們有投保旅行險的嗎？……

項……有，……什麼險，都有。（說著打開皮包）唔……桑董事長，……這兒有一份完整的資料，……你可以先看一看！……（交資料給父看）

正……爸，……你讓他走算了，……何必跟他嚕囌呢？……

父……人有旦夕禍福，……保個險，……也是保障一份安全。……

項……對……極了，……桑董事長，……真是說得，對……對極了。……

父……這樣吧！……我保……一千萬，……可以嗎？……

項……（大吃一驚）一千萬？……保多少天呢？

父……要不要體格檢查？

項：要……董……事長，……這是高額保險，一定要體格檢查的。

父：好吧，……那投保一千萬，三十天，我要交多少保費？……

項：這……這……我要算一算！……（取出計算器……計算了一下）一天是……壹千零柒拾元，卅天，應該是三萬貳千壹百元……

父：是這麼多嗎？

項：（忽想起）對……不起，……我弄錯了……應該只收肆千貳佰壹拾柒元……

父：怎麼？又這麼少了呢？……

項：我……再算一遍！……（再打計算機，一遍又一遍）我弄錯了，有優待規定。

父：好了，……好了，……明天，……你去我公司，……找丁秘書，……弄清楚了，在走以前，我作完體格檢查，就開支票給你，……我現在……還有別的事，……要辦！……

項：好……董事長，……真……好……

父：（對正說）你送他出去。……

正：項先生，……請吧！……

項：再見。……（走到門口，忽又折還）對……了……我……說的肆千貳百壹拾柒元……沒有錯！……一個月，有優待，一……點……兒也沒錯……。

（項還未說完，正已將之推出門外）

父：（莞爾一笑）……這樣的寶貝，……還出來拉保險！……

（這時，德正送走了項，却引了馬太太進屋）

正：爸，……姑媽來看你了！……

馬：表哥，……我聽說：德芬被綁票了，是眞的嗎？……現在，……怎麼樣了！……有沒有去報警呀？……

父：我沒有報警，……也沒有跟他們討價還價，……把錢要我太太給他們送去，……已經整整三天了，……換來換去，不知道換了多少個地方了，……就是沒有看見他們的人露面，來把錢拿去！……

馬：他們一定以爲你已報了警，……所以，才不敢露面！……

父：淑貞，……那你說，……我該怎麼辦呢？……我眞擔心急死了，德芬，會不會……已經遭了他的毒手？……

馬：我想……不會吧？……

父：這很難說，……有些歹徒，不是明明把人都弄死了，……還向家屬開口要錢呢！……唉！……這是什麼社會！……人心怎麼會變得這麼可怕！……

正：爸，……你冷靜一下，……我想，……我們還是應該去報警，……至少治安單位，……可以幫我們的忙，……

父：「報警」、「報警」，……你就知道去報警！……除了這一招，……你還有什麼更好的主意？……
……

馬：表哥，……我有個主意，……你願不願聽？

父：什麼主意？……你說呀！

馬：前幾天，……我爲了親戚的一批私貨，被海關扣留了要充公，來找你幫忙，你不肯。……後來，……有一個朋友，介紹我去找周委員，……想不到，……他只給我打了個電話，……問題就解決了，……這年頭，……眞是有錢，也不一定什麼都能行得通，……要有權有勢，……才吃得開。

父：淑貞，……難道，……要綁匪「放人」，……周委員也可以辦得到嗎？

馬：呀！（得意的）現在，……可是你來求我啦？……可眞是難得喲！……

父：淑貞，……看你的面子，……周委員，會肯答應幫這個忙嗎？……

正：爸，……那就請姑媽，……要周委員，……也幫我們一個忙，……把妹妹早一點放回家來！

父：淑貞，……我急得……人都快發瘋了，……你還說這樣的話！

（電話鈴響，德正去接聽）

正：喂！……我就是德正，……你是莉莉？……我……現在沒有空，……改天……再和你聯絡！……

（急將電話掛上）

三五

父：德正，……是誰打電話來？……

馬：女朋友，是不是？……

父：叫什麼「莉莉」，……準不是什麼正經女人，……德正，……爸不干涉你談戀愛，……但是，…
…千萬別拈花惹草，……交些不三不四的女人，……給自己添麻煩，知道嗎？……

正：爸，……我……自己會小心的！……

父：那就好，……淑貞，……德芬被綁票的事，……你說的那位周委員，他真能幫得上忙嗎？……

馬：我朋友說，……他是「萬事通」，不論什麼事，……黑道、白道的，他都有辦法解決！……

父：好，……淑貞，那你就幫我一個忙，……請周委員出馬，……去疏通一下，若是他真能讓德芬，
早一點平安的放回來，……我一定會好好的包一個「紅包」送給他。……

馬：表哥，……你準備送他多少？……

父：（考慮了一下）一千萬，可不可以？……

馬：我……先去找他說說看，……再來給你回音！……

父：淑貞，……那……我就把希望，全放在你身上了。……

馬：自己人，……別再客氣了，……我現在就去找周委員！……

（馬起身離去，下）

父：（起立）唉，……「破財消災！」……就怕，破了財，……還不一定消得了災。……

正：爸，……你已經三天三夜沒有睡了，……要不要上樓去休息一下，……我在這兒守著電話，……

不走開！……

父：唉，……我是想休息，……可是，……怎麼放得下這個心呢！

（阿香自外提菜籃子上）

父：阿香，你回來了！

正：香，……你回來了？

香：少爺，太太，小姐，……她們還沒回來？

正：沒有，……

香：（發現桌上，未喝的牛奶、吐司）老爺，……你早點也沒有吃？……

父：我吃不下，……你收走吧！……

香：是，……老爺。……（阿香把早點放入冰箱後，再提菜籃入廚房下）

（屋外傳來汽車喇叭聲）

父：（欣喜）啊，……是你媽回來了？……

正：對，……是老黃的喇叭。……（去開門）

正：德正，快去開門。……

父：（欣喜）啊，……德正回來了。……

正：……沒錯。……（去開門）

（停了一會兒，德正扶著衰弱的母親，自外上，司機老黃在後，拿了個大哥大，跟之進入客廳）

父：太太，……你的臉色好難看，……是不是不舒服？……錢送走啦？

母：嗯！……我的心……跳得好厲害，……炳成，……我想上樓去躺一下。

父‥德正，……快扶你媽上樓去休息，……引發了心臟病，可不得了。

正‥是……（正扶母上樓去）

父‥老黃，……那一袋子錢，……他們收下了嗎？

黃‥董事長，……為了送這包錢，……我兜了快三個多鐘頭，……後來，他們用大哥大和太太聯繫，要我們在汐止交流道把這袋子錢，放在第一個電線桿下面，……我們就離開了。……

父‥這麼說，……他們應該是拿到錢了！……那什麼時候放人呢？

黃‥董事長，……他們在電話裡說，……錢到手三個鐘頭以後，……他們一定放人，……他們絕對說話算話的！……

父‥老黃，……但願他們真的「說話算話」，就好了。

黃‥董事長，……你今天還去不去公司？

父‥你也累了，……去休息一下，……我不去公司，……我先上樓去瞇下眼睛，……希望，小姐，……等一下，真能平安回來。……

黃‥是，董事長。……（出門去，下）

（德正下樓來）

正‥爸，……你去陪陪媽吧！……

父‥好。……（上樓去以前，叮囑）德正，……你在客廳守著，……別隨便離開。……（上樓入臥室

三八

正‥是。

（這時，德昌背著書包自外進入）

正‥小弟，……你怎麼啦，放學啦！……

昌‥我有點不舒服，……請了假回來休息的！……

正‥要不要緊？……

昌‥哥，……姐……回來了沒有？……

正‥還沒有。……

昌‥我去房裡睡一下，……中午別叫我吃飯了。……

正‥好。

（德昌入自己臥室下）

（正拿起一枝煙來抽，稍頃，電話鈴響）

正‥（接聽）喂，……我是德正，……莉莉，……我不是說，現在沒空，走不開嗎？……什麼？……你……生氣了，……今天，……是你的生日，……要是我不出來，和你見面，……你就再也不理我了。……莉莉，……你聽我說，……我妹妹還沒回家，……我……實在，……不便出來了！……

……（對方掛斷電話聲）喂，……嗳喲，……怎麼把電話掛斷了呢？……（放下話筒）

三九

（德正在屋內來回徘徊，像是一熱鍋上的螞蟻一般。稍頃，阿香自內出，正如獲救星）

正：阿香，……你不出去吧？

香：少爺，有什麼事嗎？

正：我有要緊的事，需要出去一下，……要是我父親下樓來問起，……你……就說，我有些不舒服，……出去看醫生去了，知道嗎？

香：好，……少爺，你眞的有些不舒服嗎？……

正：假的啦！……你……可不能說出來噢！……我走了！……（走了一半，阿香將之叫住）……

香：少爺，回不回來吃飯？……

正：不一定，……也許，……很快就回來。……

香：準，……又是去會女朋友了。……

（正開門出去，下）

香：好啦，……我知道啦！

（香入廚房下，空場片刻）

（稍頃，德昌拿一杯子，自自己房中走出，在客廳倒了一杯水，手在發抖，還沒喝到口，手一鬆，杯子掉在地上，打碎了。）

昌：怎麼搞的，……我的手，竟然連杯子也拿不住了，……不吃藥，……會這麼難受！……！（又打

四〇

噴嚏，流鼻涕）我眞熬不下去了。

（阿香聞聲自內出，關心的上前問）

香：小少爺，……你怎麼啦？……是不是病了？

昌：誰說我病了？……我沒有病！

香：那……你怎麼臉色這麼難看，……你在發抖，……天氣並不冷嘛！……

昌：我的頭好痛，……你走開，別來煩我，好不好？……（二手抱著頭，痛苦地）想不到，……要戒掉他，……會這麼難過？……
（痛恨的自己摃打自己）……

香：小少爺，……你究竟是怎麼回事？……你不舒服，……我打電話去找醫生來！給你看一看，好不好？

昌：我……不是病，……用不著找醫生來。……（又連連打噴嚏，忽跌倒在地上，……掙扎著爬起來，……）我眞受不了了，我的頭痛，肚子也不舒服，又怕冷，又出冷汗，……阿香，……拜託你快給我去買包藥，好不好？……我實在受不了了，……我快要死了，活不下去了！……

香：小少爺，……你是受了涼，重感冒，是不是？……我這就給你去買感冒特效藥，吃了很快就會好的！……

昌：阿香，……不是治感冒的藥，……是能夠救我命的藥，……求你，……快……救救我……我……

現在，……比死還要難過！……

香：難道，……你……是在吸毒，……你要我去給你買「阿非他命」，是不是？小少爺，……你這麼年輕，就吸上了毒癮？……

昌：不是「阿非他命」。你別弄錯了！……

香：那……是「速賜康」？

昌：也不是「速賜康」。

香：是「紅中」？還是「白板」！

昌：不是的，……不是的，……是「嗎啡」！……

香：（訝異地）啊！……「嗎啡」！……到那兒去買？

昌：在慈安宮過去五十公尺左右，有一個小巷子，巷子口，有一個賣雙冬檳榔的老太婆，她那兒有的買！……你拿二千塊錢給她，給她做一個這樣的手勢（伸出大姆指及食指）她就會拿一個白紙包給你，……快去，……你聽清楚了沒有？

香：什麼？兩千塊錢買一包，這麼貴啊！

昌：別再囉嗦了，……我實在熬不過去了，……真沒有想到，要戒掉這鬼東西，會這麼受不了！……

香：小少爺，你好好的，怎麼會染上吸嗎啡的毛病呢！

昌：唉！……我都是讓同學他們害的，……起先，吸著好玩，……誰知道，會上了癮呢！……好了，

別再說什麼廢話了，你快去給我買啊！

香：好，……我這就去給你買！……那錢呢？

昌：我現在沒有錢，你先墊一下，不行啊？

香：先墊一墊？

昌：等一下，……我找我媽要了，……一定會還你的，……你放心好了！

香：好了，……我給你墊就是了！……

昌：快去快回，……阿香，……你給我買嗎啡的事，千萬別讓我媽知道了！……聽見了沒有？……

香：聽見了。

（這時樓上，母開了房門走出，注意聽樓下德昌與阿香的說話，但德昌與阿香並不知道）

昌：若是讓我媽知道了，……那就嘮叨個沒完沒了了。……

母：阿香，……你要到那兒去？

香：（一楞）……我……去給小少爺……買藥。

母：去給小少爺……買藥去。

香：好了，……別說了，……我走了。

（母喝住，並快步走下樓梯）

昌：阿香，……我走了。

母：買什麼藥？……

昌：特效藥，……治感冒的特效藥！媽，……你沒看見我在流鼻水，又冒冷汗嗎？……我的頭，痛得

快要裂開似的！……媽，……你讓阿香快去吧！

母：德昌，……你真想把媽給矇在鼓裡是不是？……剛剛我明明聽你在和阿香說：「你給我買嗎啡的

事，千萬別讓我媽知道了……」我沒有聽錯吧！

昌：媽——

母：德昌，……你……怎麼小小年紀，就會染上了毒癮呢？……要是讓你爸知道了，……他也許會氣

的把你趕出門去的！……

昌：媽，……我……知道錯了，……我是在想戒掉它，……誰知道，……會這麼難過呢？……

母：你……這兩天，……的神色，……我就覺得不對！……我還以為你是不是病了！……想不到，你

居然……染上了這樣的惡習！……若是戒不掉，……你這一輩子，就完了，……你知不知道？……

昌：媽，……你別罵了，……乾脆！……（大聲）拿把刀，把我殺了算了，……我……受不了，……我……

……恨不得現在，……就死在你的面前。（蹲在地上，痛苦的用力自己搥打自己的頭）

母：（抱住德昌）德昌，……媽……完全是為了你好，才罵你，（無奈地）好吧，既然你這麼痛苦，

……阿香，……先去給他買一包再說，……明天，……我……親自送他去煙毒勒戒所，……非把

「毒癮」戒掉不可！……

香：太太，……那我去了！……（下）

昌：快去，……（嘶喊）我等著它來救我的命！……

母：德昌，……媽沒有好好管教你，……害你變成這樣！……媽的心理，比你還難過！……那些天殺的「黑心鬼」，什麼錢不好賺，偏偏要運那些毒品進來，害人，……老天爺，……你若長了眼睛，……你讓他們，不得好死！……

父：太太，……（在樓梯上說，邊說邊走下來）……你在和誰說話，大聲嚷嚷的，把我吵醒了，……是不是德芬，……已經被他們放回來了？

（這時，樓上的臥室門開了，父穿晨樓走出，走下樓來）

母：你醒了？……德芬，還沒有回來！……剛才，是德昌有點感冒，我要他去看醫生，他不肯，我已

父：啊！……德昌，……我看你學校的成績很不好，……要不要爸爸給你請個家庭教師，……給你補習功課！……

昌：爸，不用了。……我很不舒服，……我想回房去休息一下。……

父：也好，……你去吧！……太太，你看要不要找醫生到家來，給他看一看。

（昌入自己臥室，下）

母：不用了，……吃了藥，……大概就會好的！

父：……（看錶）唉，……你錢送去到現在，已經三個多小時了，……怎麼還不見德芬回來呢！……萬一

，他們不守信用，……我們這五千萬，不是白送了嗎！……

母：還是德正說得對，……炳成，……我們是該去報警的！報了警，治安當局會幫我們想辦法破案，現在……這些歹徒……也實在太可惡了！……怎麼可以拿了錢，還不放人回來呢？

父：德正，他人呢？……我要他守在家裡的，……怎麼不見人呢？……德正！（去打開德正房間的門，看了一下，又關上）嘿！……準又出去會女朋友去了。……

（這時，老黃引德芬面色憔悴，十分疲憊，穿同第一幕之服裝上）

黃：董事長，……大小姐，……她回來了。……

母：德芬，……你……回來啦？……

芬：（見了母親，停步下來，再激動的衝上前去，投入母懷，與母相擁後大哭）媽——，……

母：孩子，……回來就好了，……別哭了。……

父：老天爺，……總算這些歹徒，……還有些三天良。……德芬，……告訴爸，……他們沒有欺侮你吧？……

芬：（見父走近，如驚弓之鳥似的，歇斯的里的叫著）別靠近我，你再走近一步，……我就和你拚了。……

母：德芬，……別緊張，……他不是壞人，他是你爸爸，……你不認識他了？

芬：（迷惘地，走近父）……你是……爸爸？……你真的是我爸爸？不……（退後）……你在騙我，……

……你……想騙我上當！……

父：德芬，……爸爸，……怎麼會騙你吶？……好，……你先坐下，……你四周看一看，……你已經平安回家來了，……這……沙發，……桌子，椅子，……你都記不起來了嗎？……

芬：（懷疑地）我……真的回家來了嗎？……（四周打量，摸著沙發及傢俱）嗯，……不錯，……這是……我的家！……他們真的放我回家來了！……

父：德芬，……你失去自由，已經七十二小時以上了，……他們有沒有給你吃東西，有沒有打你，……不讓你睡覺？……你說給爸爸聽，好不好？……

芬：（呼天搶地的嚎叫）爸爸……（投入父懷）嗚……（哭泣不已，說不出一句話來）

父：孩子，……爸知道你吃了不少苦，……受了不少的罪！……難道，我的女兒，平白無辜，就該受這樣的罪嗎？……

母：炳成，……我看，眼前，她情緒一時還不能平靜下來，……還是先讓我陪她回房去，休息一下，再慢慢說吧！

父：也好。……（放開德芬，讓她給母親）
（這時，阿香，引著梁院長自外進入）

香：老爺，愛愛孤兒院的梁院長來看你。……

父：啊！……梁院長請坐。……

香：（看見德芬）啊，……太太，……小姐已經放回來啦？

母：嗯！……她太疲倦了，……我扶她上房裡去，先睡一下，再說。……對了，……阿香，……你給小少爺買的藥，買到了嗎？

香：買到了，……唔，……在這兒。……（將藥給母看）

母：是藥房配的！（將藥交給阿香）快給小少爺送去，伺候他吃下，多喝點開水。

父：什麼特效藥，拿來我看看。……（欲將藥取去，被母搶去了）

香：（接藥）時！……（即入德昌臥室，下）

母：梁院長，我送她回房去休息，失陪啦！……

梁：桑太太，別客氣，你忙。……

（母親進入她的臥室，下）

（父這時自己倒了杯水，送給梁院長）

父：梁院長，今天來，有什麼事嗎？……若需要我幫忙的，請儘管開口，就是了。

梁：董事長，剛才我來的時候，在門口聽阿香說，……你小姐被人綁票了，……是真的嗎？

父：對，她是被人綁了票，……我們付了錢，對方，才把她放回來的！……唉呀，……這幾天……我和太太，急得三天三夜都沒睡好覺！……現在，人回來了，才鬆了口氣，放下了一付重擔！

梁：噢，……那真是做了好事有好報，吉人自有天相，……恐怕化了不少錢吧？

父：只要人能平安回來，就好了！……就怕，有時，破了財，還消不了災！那才冤枉呢！

梁：董事長，……像你這樣熱心公益的慈善家，……不可能破了財，還消不了災的！……

父：梁院長今天來，……是不是又需要……我再捐一點錢？……你說就是了，……我不會拒絕的！

梁：董事長，別誤會，我今天來，不是來要董事長捐錢的。……是這樣的，本院這一次，重新擴建院舍，蒙董事長慷慨解囊，現在，已經大功告成，我們院裡選定了下個月五號，舉行新院舍的啓用典禮。……這是一份請帖！（說著打開皮包，拿出一份請帖交給父）

父：（看了一下請帖）啊，下個月五號？……

梁：我特別代表全體的院童，恭請董事長親自光臨，爲我們剪綵，做我們的貴賓。

父：梁院長，你自己來主持剪綵，不很好嗎？何必要我來剪綵呢？

梁：董事長，我說實在話，本院這幾年來，要不是您大力支持，也許早就不存在了，所以，這一次新院舍的啓用典禮，您非抽空來主持不可，再沒有別人，比你更恰當了！

父：梁院長，你這樣誠意的邀請，我是應該來參加，可是下個月五號，我可能人還在泰國，趕不回來，……很難答應你呀！

梁：董事長，最近，要去泰國？

父：我是去接洽一些生意上的事情，……這樣吧，……要是趕的回來，……我就來剪綵，要是趕不回來，……就只有另請高明了。……

梁：董事長既然這麼說，那就確定這樣了。……另外還有一件事，我也向董事長報告一下，……就是社會局方面，要我們提報本年度「好人好事」的名單，好報請上級擴大表揚，我已經把董事長的名字，及具體的事實，呈報上去了，希望這一次，董事長勿再辭謝推却。

父：梁院長，我一再給你說，……我不是一個沽名釣譽的人，我捐助貴院經費，也只是表示一點我回饋社會的心意，千萬不要把我列入「好人好事」的名單；至於接受擴大表揚，更是我擔待不起的事！

梁：董事長，你何必這麼謙虛，客氣呢？

父：梁院長，絕不是我謙虛、客氣。古人說：「為善不欲人知」，我捐的錢，也都用「無名氏」的名義，……我誠懇的請求你，務必撤銷我的名字，……要是你不肯這樣做，……那我今後，就不再捐助了。

梁：董事長，真是這樣堅持嗎？……

父：我是真心的，梁院長，無論如何，希望你接受我撤銷的請求。說真的，我做善事，只是求「心安」，我算不得是個值得表揚的「好人」。

梁：董事長，既然這麼說，那我也不便再勉強了，不過，董事長這種胸懷，真是令人衷心欽佩。……

好了，我回去以後，馬上和社會局的主辦人說明，把你的名字予以註銷。

父：謝謝梁院長，你的一番好意，我心領了。……謝謝。

梁：該謝的，是我才對。董事長，那我告辭了，……再見。

父：再見，……不送你了，梁院長。

（梁向大門口走去，下）

父：阿香！……

（阿香自德昌房中出）

香：老爺，你是不是要出去？我去叫老黃把車開出來！

父：等一下，我才出去，你先幫我去沖杯咖啡，送到書房裡來。

香：是，老爺。（去沖咖啡，在場上沖就可以了）

（父進入書房，先打開燈，再打開保險箱，取出一些文件，仔細的看著，阿香將咖啡送入後退出，父喝著咖啡，抽著煙斗，在盤算著）

（門鈴響，阿香去開門，不久引大成進入客廳）

香：姪少爺，……老爺在書房裡，……你請坐，我去通知他。……

成：不用了，……我去書房見他。（成進入書房）二叔。……

父：大成，……你來了。

成：……剛才才回家來！……

父：送了五千萬，……

成：德芬被綁票，放回來了沒有？（阿香送上茶後，退出，下）

成‥能平安回來，‥‥‥還算不幸中的大幸。‥‥‥

父‥大成，‥‥‥美國方面的人來了沒有？

成‥來了，現在，在來來格里拉，‥‥‥等著聽你的回音！

父‥大成，‥‥‥剛才，我一個人，仔細考慮了好久，‥‥‥這筆生意，‥‥‥我想放棄，不做了。

成‥爲什麼呢！明擺著可以賺「上億」的生意，‥‥‥你怎麼忽然又想不做了呢？

父‥我‥‥‥覺得‥‥‥最近運氣，很不順，‥‥‥我怕‥‥‥會出事情！

成‥二叔，‥‥‥我是你的親姪子，你說，‥‥‥我怎麼會害你呐！‥‥‥唔‥‥‥（身上取出一份電報）美國的電報，我剛收到，‥‥‥你看，‥‥‥他們也希望做成這筆生意。

父‥（看了電報，陷入矛盾的掙扎）大成，‥‥‥這筆交易，‥‥‥做成了，‥‥‥我們眞可以分到三億多的利潤？

成‥也許還不止呢？‥‥‥二叔，‥‥‥德芬的事，‥‥‥讓你平空丟了五千萬，‥‥‥你總得想法子，找地方補回來呀！‥‥‥做貿易生意，只要膽大心細，‥‥‥穩賺不賠的。‥‥‥上一回，我們只是小做了一下，‥‥‥不就賺了不少嗎？‥‥‥

父‥話是不錯，‥‥‥不過，我總覺得凡事，還是小心謹愼最重要，所謂不怕一萬，就怕萬一，‥‥‥你要知道，我在社會上，是有身份、地位的人，‥‥‥可千萬不能摔筋斗啊！‥‥‥你

成‥二叔，你別說了，我會替你守秘密的，眞要有了麻煩，我人在美國，他們又能怎麼樣？‥‥‥放心

好了，……二叔，絕對，錯不了。

父：（猶豫難決）……真是這樣嗎？……

成：二叔，……現在時代變了，潮流也在變，……我們的想法，也該跟着變，才能生存下去啊！

父：真非變不可嗎？

成：美國人常說：「凡事要跑在別人前面，老跟在別人的汽車後面去追，只有去聞臭氣……」

父：大成，……明天，你就回美國去？……

成：是啊！……就打長途電話給你。……二叔，……你出錢，我出力，賺了好處，……我們還是五五對分唷！

父：大成，……你先去來來香格里拉，……跟史密斯先生聊一聊，……我還有些雜事，處理好了，馬上就去。

成：二叔，……別三心二意，猶豫不決了，……機會像匹馬，來了，就得伸手把它抓住。……我先走了。

父：好，……我一會兒，就到。……（將文件放回保險箱去）

（成自書房出，獨自開門離去）

父：（鎖上保險箱才走出書房，……躊躇徘徊了一陣，忽見母，哭腫了臉，自女兒德芬房中走出）太，……你怎麼啦？……

母：（大聲哭出，衝向父親）炳成，……咱們的女兒，……德芬，……給……他們……毀了！……

父：什麼？（驚駭）毀了？……

母：他們先是把她蒙上了眼睛、嘴巴，把她關在一間黑屋子裡，不給她喝水，也不給她飯吃！……到了半夜，才給她一個麵包，一杯果汁，……德芬喝了那杯果汁，……就昏沉沉睡了過去，什麼都不知道了，……

父：那一定是在果汁裡，掺了安眠藥！或是「麻醉品」！……

母：第二天德芬醒來，……睡在床上，……發覺沒有穿褲子，……她大聲掙扎哭起來，……看守的人，才給她把褲子穿上，……炳成，……這些流氓，不單要了「錢」，……還要了「人」！……這

筆賬，我們怎麼去找他們要回來！……

父：（大怒，咆哮著說）王八蛋！……連禽獸都不如！……這樣傷天害理的事，他們都做得出來！……

⋮

（阿香聞大聲咆哮，自內走出）

香：太太，……發生了什麼事？……

母：阿香！……不關你的事，……你去忙你的！……

父：阿香，……去告訴老黃，把車子開出來，……（看錶）我馬上要出去！

母：你要去那裡？（阿香下）

父：來來香格里拉，……和美國人談一筆生意，……晚飯不可能回來吃了，……不用等我。……（邊

說脫下晨褸，換穿西裝上衣，打領帶）

母：炳成，……你說德芬的事，……怎麼辦？……

父：先不要隨便張揚出去，好好的安慰她一下，……（頓首搥足）唉，……事情已經發生了，……還

有什麼辦法好補救呢？……

母：真沒有想到，……我們做了不少的好事，結果我們的女兒，……會碰上這樣不幸的事情。……

（正說時，德正自外歸來）

正：我只是，出去一下下。……

父：（正色的）你到那兒去了？……家裡發生了這樣的事，你還有心情，出去會女朋友！……

正：爸，……媽，妹妹，放回來了沒有？……

父：（對正說）好好在家就著，別再隨便出去走動，……說不定，下一回綁票的對象，就是你！……

香：老爺，……老黃已經準備好了，……你上車吧！……

（阿香自外入）

母：德正，……你爸說的沒錯，……以後出門，還是小心一點，比較好。……

正：媽，……妹妹人呢？……我去看看她！……

母‧不用了，……別去打擾她，……讓她好好休息一下。……

正‧媽，……我給你看樣東西，……是剛才……托朋友買給我的。

母‧什麼東西？

正‧（自懷中掏出一把手槍）咭，……我買了一把「手鎗」，……放在身邊，……自衞，……以後，

就不怕歹徒，來綁我的票了！

母‧（大聲）什麼？……你買了支「手鎗」？

香‧（好奇的）啊，……大少爺，……你在那兒買的？……貴不貴？

（小弟聞聲自屋內走出）

昌‧什麼？大哥，……你買了支「手鎗」？……是「玩具手鎗」？還是眞的手鎗！

正‧當然是眞的手鎗，裡面還有子彈，可不是好玩的！

昌‧大哥，……給我看看嗎！……

正‧看看可以，……可別亂扣板機呀！……走了火，……可就麻煩了。（正將手鎗給昌，昌拿來仔細

把玩著）

（德芬這時自臥室走出）

芬‧大哥，……你買的手鎗，給我看一看，好嗎？……

正‧妹妹，……那些歹徒，……他們有沒有欺侮你？……

芬：（眼光異樣的，不作回答，向小弟說）小弟，……你把鎗給我看看嘛！……

昌：好！……給你看！（將手鎗交給德芬）別扣板機，裡面有子彈！……

芬：（接鎗在手）什麼？手鎗裡裝了子彈？……（突歇斯底裡的笑了起來）哈……哈……好極了，……

……我正不想活了，……讓我一鎗把自己打死算了！……

母：（大驚叫）德芬，……千萬別開鎗，……把鎗給我！聽見了沒有？（其餘眾人也緊張萬分）

香：小姐，……你不能死呀！

正：妹妹，……別開鎗，這不是好鬧著玩的！

昌：姊姊，……你怎麼會想到自殺呢？……把鎗還給我，早知道你要這樣，……我就不會把鎗給你了！

芬：媽，……我真的不想活了，……請你原諒我這不孝的女兒，……來世，再報答你的恩情，好不好！

母：德芬，……你要死，媽也跟你一起死！……媽也不想活了！……

正：妹妹，……你別做糊塗事，好不好？……

昌：姊！……（欲上前奪鎗，未奪下，結果鎗走火，「砰」的一聲，子彈向空中射出，正上前，才把鎗搶過來，解除了危機！）

芬：小弟，……為什麼，不讓我死呢？……

母：德芬，……你要勇敢的活下去，……聽媽的話，……好不好？……

正：妹妹，……你已經回來了，爲什麼還要尋死呢？……

（燈黑）

　　　　　　　　　　　　　　　　　　　　——幕下。

# 第三幕

幕啓時：

（第一場）

人：桑炳成、桑太太、桑德正、桑德昌、桑德芬、阿香、老黃、桑大成、項必均、梁院長、馬淑貞

景：桑家客廳

時：距第二幕約一個月後

臺上無人，是晚上七點多鐘，室內吊燈亮著。

稍頃，電話鈴響，桑太太自樓上下來。

阿香自內出，接聽電話。

香：大少爺不在，……尔等一下再打來，他會回來吃晚飯的！

（說完掛上電話）

母：阿香，是誰打電話來找大少爺？

香：她說她姓黃，叫小倩，在「新加坡」上班的。

母：「新加坡」上班的，……唉，不是酒女、就是舞女，……老是這樣花天酒地，……將來會有什麼出息！……

馬：表嫂，……表哥，到大陸去，回來了沒有？

（門鈴響，阿香去開門，引了馬淑貞進入）

母：說是今天回來的，……老黃已經開車去桃園機場接機去了，這回兒，還沒到家呢，大概快一個月，沒見你來了，這一陣子，在忙些什麼呢？

馬：我呀，……在做股票！……起先，倒很不錯的，……賺了好幾十萬！……誰知道，最近局勢不穩定，一連幾個跌停板，跌得我鼻青臉腫的！

（阿香倒茶後送上，退出）

母：是嗎？……

馬：我今兒來，就是想找你調些頭寸，週轉一下，……不知道，你手頭上方不方便？……

母：你需要調多少呢？……

馬：兩百萬。……

母‥你股票做這麼大啊？……

馬‥我是小戶，有些二太太，進出多是好幾千萬的呢！……

母‥淑貞，我現在手邊，可沒有這麼多現款，……這樣吧，……我要德正開張支票給你，……他一會兒就要回來了！

馬‥也好，……不過，表嫂，……這件事，……最好別讓表哥知道了，他呀，……會嘮叨個沒完沒了。

母‥我知道。……

馬‥對了，表嫂，……德芬，……現在，是不已經恢復平靜下來了！

母‥好是好了，……可是，不能受刺激，……一受刺激，……馬上精神就不正常了，……唉，……淑貞，真是造孽，……誰想到，她會遇上這樣的事呢？

馬‥現在的社會，真是和前二十年，大不相同了，早二十年，那兒聽說過什麼綁票，搶銀行的，……現在好了，大家手裡都有鎗，打死警察，也不算稀奇的事了，……真是太可怕了。……

母‥更要命的，是不知那裡運進來那些毒品，……什麼阿非他命、嗎啡、海洛英，……什麼都可以買得到，……一旦吸上了癮，怎麼戒也戒不掉，……真是害死人哪！……

馬‥表嫂，……我聽說，你們家德昌，也染上了毒癮，是不是真的？……

母‥（頓足）哎，真是…「好事不出門，壞事傳千里」，……淑貞，……你是聽誰說的呢？……

馬：我兒子在學校裡，聽同學說的啊，……聽說，吸毒的，還不止就德昌一個呢？……有些同學，還靠賣毒品來賺錢呢！……

母：現在的學校教育，怎麼會變成這樣！……淑貞，這件事，他父親還不知道，你千萬別告訴他知道，……趁他出國去不在家，……我已經送他去煙毒勒戒所了，……希望他能把毒癮戒掉才好。……

馬：唉，……時代真是不同了。

（此時，長子德正自外進入。）

正：媽，……姑媽，……你來啦？媽，爸……回來了沒有？

母：還沒有呢？

正：（看錶）都快八點了，爸應該到家了啊！

母：大概是高速公路塞車吧！……德正，……你先給我開一張兩百萬的支票，給你姑媽，……她有急用。

正：好。……（拿出支票簿，開支票）姑媽，……要不要抬頭？還是劃線。

馬：德正，……不用抬頭，劃線好了，……明天的期。……

正：（寫好支票，交給馬）姑媽，……小心收好，……別掉了。……

馬：德正，……謝謝你，……下個月，……我就會還給你的，……表嫂，我……回去了。……（起立）

母：淑貞，……不等你表哥回來，吃了飯再走？

六一

馬‥不了，……表嫂，德正，再見。（出門而去，下）

（德芬自臥室走出）

芬‥媽，……爸怎麼還不回來呢？我肚子好餓啊！……

母‥他自己打電報回來說，他今天會準時回家來吃晚飯的，……他還說，買了不少大陸的土產，要送給你們呢！……奇怪，……（看看錶）八點都過了，會不會他坐的飛機，出了事？

芬‥不會的，媽，……你怎麼突然想到飛機會出事，……這是不可能發生的事。

母‥昨天晚上，我做了個奇怪的夢，……夢見你爸爸，突然揮手跟我說：「再見」，我一驚，就醒了，我覺得，這是個「不祥之兆」。

芬‥媽，你真會胡思亂想，爸身體好得很，又常做好事，他不會有什麼意外的。

母‥那怎麼過了八點，還不到家呢？會不會出了車禍？……明天，是他的生日，……他走的時候，答應我，一定回家來過生日的，德芬，你也聽見的。

芬‥爸的生日禮物，我都準備好了，……哥，不是老黃去桃園機場接機的嗎……若是誤了時間，他也該先打個電話來，讓我們放心啊！……

母‥就是說！……老黃也老糊塗了。……

（門鈴響）

母‥阿香快去開門，準是老爺回來了。……

（阿香出去，沒有多久，大成隨之入，形色匆忙）

母：大成，……你從美國回來啦？

成：嗯！二嬸！二叔，從大陸回來了沒有？

母：說是今天回來，可是，到現在還沒到家。……

成：二嬸，……我現在急著辦一些事，明天就回美國去，沒時間等他，……

母：什麼？你才到，又急著走？

成：嗯，二嬸，……二叔，你跟他說，我從美國押運回來的那批貨，已經到了，貨櫃現在被扣在海關，聽說要檢查，也許會有些「麻煩」，……二叔，不妨想法子去疏通一下。……我走了，過幾天，我在美國會主動打長途電話和他聯絡的，……要他別找我！……德正、德芬，……再見。

（大成說完話，匆匆離去，下）

母：奇怪，大成，是怎麼啦？……

芬：媽，大成哥說，美國運來的貨，扣在海關，會有一些「麻煩」，那會有什麼麻煩呢！

母：不用操心，……你爸，他會有辦法解決的。……

正：奇怪，爸又不收藏古董，從美國運古董來做什麼？……

六三

（門鈴響，阿香去開門，不久是德昌回來了，阿香跟入）

芬：小弟，……你不是在「煙毒勒戒所」嗎？……你怎麼跑回來了，……毒癮，已經戒絕了嗎？……

昌：沒有，……我是逃出來的！

母：你……逃出來的，……你不想戒了？……

昌：媽？……那個勒戒所，把我關在房間裡，……就像關監牢似的，我受不了，……我是利用上廁所的時候，爬牆偷跑出來的，……阿香，快……再給我去買包藥，……我的毒癮，又快發作了！……

母：……你……阿香，快……看他怎麼樣！

昌：媽，……你……真這麼狠心，看我難過得在地上打滾嗎？……好，……不買就不買！……我……

正：小弟，……你這樣子，一輩子也戒不了了！……

昌：阿香，……你快去買嗎？……

（阿香不動，徵求母的意思，要不要去買？）

母：不要去買！……

昌：……你……

（昌欲衝出去，阿香將他攔住）

這就去死在外面，……你們再也不要管我！

母：……去死，……好，……不買就不買！……我……

香：小少爺，別再這樣，……太太，……也是為了你好！……

昌：（毒癮發作）噢，……我的頭又痛起來了，……（又打噴嚏）……（走向媽，跪下）媽，……你

真願意，看我這樣難過嗎？……

芬：媽，……你就答應他吧！……

正：媽，……暫時，……先讓他過了癮，再說。

母：（無法再堅持）阿香，……你就去買一包給他。……（哭泣著說）孩子，……是誰造的孽，……讓你沾上了毒癮！戒也戒不掉。

（阿香出，眾人也鬆了口氣）

母：德芬，……扶他到房裡去，……別讓你爸回家來，……看到這樣的場面，……

芬：是，媽。……（芬扶德昌進自己臥室）

（電話鈴響）

正：（去接聽）喂，……是老黃，在機場打回來的！……

母：（接聽電話）來，……老黃，你說什麼？……

黃：（把電話中的聲音，用迴聲擴大）太太，……老爺搭的那班，從泰國起飛的飛機，……因為機件發生故障，出事了，……死了不少旅客，受傷的也不少，……老爺正巧就在這飛機上，……生死傷亡，現在還不知道，……

母：老黃，……快去航空公司，把名單查清楚，……有什麼消息，馬上打電話回來！……（手一鬆，話筒掉落地上）

芬……（緊張）媽，……你鎮靜一點，……爸也許不在名單上！……媽，你別哭嘛！……（也跟著哭起來）

正……媽，……爸，……做了一輩子好事，……他不會出事的！……

母……德芬，……快去把萬金油，給我拿來，……我的頭好疼，……

芬……是。（急忙翻找抽屜，找出萬金油，給媽搽著）

母……炳成，……是個好人，……吉人自有天相，……我想老天爺，會保佑他，不會橫死的！……

（燈黑，暗轉）

（第二場）

（燈再亮時，牆上已掛上了桑炳成的遺像，悲愴的音樂升起，阿香在靈堂前燒紙錢，老黃點上香燭向遺像叩頭）

黃……（叩完頭起立）……唉，……真沒有想到，董事長生前做了那麼多的善事，……却落得這麼個下場！……

香……真是做夢也想不到的事，……老爺，……就這樣，說走就走了，……太太還說，她做了個夢，夢見老爺和她揮手說：「再見」，想不到，真應驗了！……

黃……阿香，這年頭，想不到的事，……還多著呢？……你看，董事長生前，來看他的人，左一批、右一批的，……現在，人死了，真是連個「鬼」，也不上門來了！……

香：老黃，別再說什麼「死」呀「鬼」呀的，……我聽了都害怕！……

黃：好，……我不說，……對了，……，小姐學校快放學了，……我得開車去接她呢！……自從，董

事長出事以後，我看她，神情有點怪怪的，……希望別再出什麼「意外」！……

香：你說小姐神情怪怪的，……難道，她又想「自殺」了！

黃：嗯，……有這個「可能」，……你呀，……最好多提防著她一點，太太，可不能再受什麼打擊了

！……

香：我知道了，老黃，你快走吧！……

（門鈴響）

黃：你別出去了，我去給你開門，看是誰來了！再見！（向外出，下）

（不久，梁院長自外進來）

香：喔，……梁院長來啦！……請坐，……我去請太太下來。

（梁入坐，阿香上樓，不久桑太太身上帶了孝，自樓上走下來，阿香隨著下來倒茶，為梁院長送

上後退下）

母：梁院長，……謝謝你來看我。

梁：……桑夫人，……真是想不到的事，桑董事長怎麼這麼快，就走了。院裡的孩子們，聽說桑董事長飛

（梁先向桑炳成遺像行禮後，才說話）

六七

機失事遭了難，都難過得吃不下飯，哭腫了眼睛，……桑夫人，我是特地專誠來看看你，希望你

還是多保重自己身體要緊！……

母：（哀幽地）梁院長，……謝謝你。

梁：真是想都沒有想到的事，……這樣不幸的事，怎麼可能發生在桑董事長的身上呢！（說著聲音哽

　　咽起來）老天爺，也太不公平了。……

母：人哪，……爭不過天，……這幾天，我沒有一天睡著過，老是想著他生前的一些往事，……我想

　　，……這一切，大概都是「天意」。

梁：「天意」？……桑董事長，生前做了多少善事，……說什麼，也不該，就這樣走了啊！……俗話

　　說：「善有善報，惡有惡報」，……現在這樣，不是太「善惡不分」了嗎？……

母：梁院長，……事情既然發生了，……我們也只能想開一點，要不然，又能怎麼樣呢？……

梁：桑夫人，……你能這樣想，我也就放心了。……

母：梁院長，……你也請放心，你們院裡的經費，我還是會像我先生生前一樣，定期繼續捐獻下去，

　　不會讓孩子們，餓著或是凍著，……不管怎麼說，……這些錢，我還負擔得起！

梁：桑夫人……你這樣說，真使我感動，……我真不知該怎麼謝你才好。

母：不用謝，這是做好事，……我是甘心樂意，這樣做的。

梁：桑夫人，……你沒有去泰國，料理後事？

母：我要大兒子，去辦了，……昨天，已經把骨灰，……帶回來了。……過幾天，選定了日子，再出

　　殯！

梁：桑夫人，……節哀順變，……我不打擾，……告辭了。

母：梁院長，我不送你了。……

梁：別客氣。

母：阿香，送客。

香：是。

　　（阿香送梁院長出，不久回來時，又聞門鈴響，再去開門，引馬淑貞入，馬進屋後，也默默先向

　　桑遺像行禮後，再說話）

馬：表哥，……你怎麼，什麼也沒有交待，就這樣走了呢？……留下表嫂一個人，……這往後的日子

　　怎麼過呢？（哭起來）

母：淑貞，……別哭了！……你一哭，……我也要哭了！……（抹眼睛）

馬：（忍住）好，……我不哭！……表嫂，……德正去泰國料理後事，已經回來了」沒有？

母：昨兒已經把骨灰帶回來了，……今天去看墳地去了。

馬：表哥走的時候，……我找你週轉的那兩佰萬元，……本來，昨天就到期了，……可是

　　，……我實在有困難，……可不可以再延後一個月還，……我的股票，都給套牢了！……

母：淑貞，……這些小錢，你慢慢還，不用急，……我不等著用。……

馬：（高興）表嫂，……你真好，……幫了我大忙。……

母：自己人，還說什麼客套話。……

馬：表嫂……（自皮包取出一張晚報來，給母看）……有一張晚報上，登了一段這樣的消息，……不知道，你看到了沒有？

母：什麼消息，拿來我看看！（仔細看報）……

（配強烈變化的音效）

母：什麼？……大成，……在出境的時候，……被治安機關抓起來了！……

馬：表嫂，……這是真的，還是假的？……我不敢相信吶！

母：（繼續看報）什麼？從美國運來的貨櫃，被海關打開檢查的結果，發現其中，只有一小部份，裝的是古董，其餘大部份裝的是槍枝、彈藥，還有衝鋒鎗！

馬：表嫂，表哥是正人君子，大慈善家，怎麼會做這樣不法的事情呢？……會不會是弄錯了？……

母：（繼續看報）啊！……除了「軍火」以外，還查到不少「嗎啡」「海洛因」！……（放下報紙）炳成一向說：「做人，人格最重要；做事，一定要走正路」，……他怎麼可能會去販賣軍火、毒品，……這是「不可能」的事。

馬：表嫂，……我也不敢相信，這是真的，……所以，特地來問你！……也許是報紙，無中生有，故

意造謠，……想弄點好處！……

母：（一臉茫然）炳成，……這些年來，是發了些財，他說是經濟起飛，給他帶來了「財運」，……難道，……他發的都是些「不義之財」！

馬：表嫂！（再指給母看，報上另一關欄）你看，……這邊還說，桑大成，經過偵訊，已經完全招認，……說幕後出錢的老闆，是他的二叔桑炳成，他只是被利用代為經手罷了！……

母：淑貞，……別再說了！……一定是大成，……他知道炳成飛機失事死了，……所以，才把罪過，完全推在炳成頭上，……大成怎麼可以這樣說呢？……啊……我的頭又疼起來了，……阿香，快把萬金油給我拿來。……

香：（應聲上）是，……太太。……（尋找萬金油，找到了，給母搽上）

馬：表嫂，……我還有別的事，……先走了，……改天，……再來看你。……

母：（再一次冷靜的看那張晚報，心聲用Ｏ·Ｓ方式，在幕後播出）難怪，這些年，炳成特別喜歡捐獻，做善事，……原來，他賺的都是些「黑心錢」！……「見不得人的錢」！……對了，我得把他的保險箱打開來看看，……還有什麼我不知道的秘密？

（母起立，走進書房，打開燈，再打開保險箱，把一些錢和金塊拿出來，又發現一些文件，一一仔細看著）

母‥這是什麼機密文件？……包了又包，（一邊說，一邊把包文件的紙逐一解開）啊，……原來是跟

泰國，一個公司簽訂的秘密合約，……（看了一陣，訝異的叫出聲來）什麼？……他要從泰國販

運大麻、鴉片，還有春藥、春酒到臺灣來銷售，……利潤是五五對分！……太可怕了。炳成，…

…你賺了這些錢，……死了以後，……不怕被打入地獄，上刀山、下油鍋！……（越想越害怕，

把那份合約撕個粉碎。）

（這時，德昌臂上帶黑紗自外進入，見書房燈亮著，就進入書房）

昌‥媽！……你在清理父親留下的財產？……（母沒答理他，他看見桌上有一大疊的紙幣和金塊）啊

，……好多的錢呀！……媽，你給我一點，……我最近打算自立，做生意去！……（說完自己動

手，被母阻止）

母‥不准動，……這些錢，要留給你父親辦喪事用的！……

昌‥那先給我一百萬，總可以吧，……我又不要多！

母‥給你，……給你去買「嗎啡」來吃？……

昌‥媽，……我會把毒癮戒掉的，……我已經和朋友說好了，……準備合夥做生意，媽，做生意，總

需要一些本錢，是不是？……（仍要拿錢，母阻止）……你不給錢，……給我金條，也可以啊！

……

母‥你這沒出息的東西！……我怎麼會生下你這麼不爭氣的兒子，……你給我出去！出去！

（母子爭執中，長子德正臂上戴有黑紗，面容憔悴，自外進入，聽見母大聲吆喝，進入書房）

正：媽，……我回來了，……爸的墳地已經弄好了，……小弟，……你跟媽在吵些什麼？……

母：德昌他要我給他一百萬，……他說他要去做生意！……你說我能給他嗎？

正：小弟，……你還在學校讀書，做什麼生意？……

昌：我想自立，不行嗎？……

正：你先把毒癮戒掉了再說，……我不相信，一個吸毒的人，還能夠自立！

昌：哼，別以爲你是我大哥，……就處處管著我，……我告訴你，……爸已經死了，……我要求「分家」，……你是我，我是你，……以後，誰也別管誰？……

母：德昌，……你在胡說些什麼？你爸才死，還沒出殯……你就想「分家」……我不同意！……

正：我也不同意！

母：同不同意，我不管！（說完自桌子上搶了一些錢出去）我‧現在就去找律師去！……（奪門而去）

昌：（突感不適）媽，……我的心口絞痛得很利害，……我想回房去休息！

母：（嘆息）唉，德昌，怎麼會變成這樣？……

正：這些日子，……你太累了，回房去休息一下也好！……（順手摸正的額頭）啊，……你在發燒，額頭滾燙，要不要去看醫生去？……

正：不用看醫生，……我最近常這樣，躺一下，就會好的！……

母：好吧，……你去吧！（把錢放回保險箱鎖好，關燈，走出書房）

（正入自己臥室，室外汽車喇叭聲響，阿香去開門。）

香：一定是小姐回來了。……（出去開門，不久，德芬也臂上戴黑紗上，阿香隨之入）

香：小姐，……你怎麼啦？……哭得眼睛都腫了！

母：德芬，……是誰欺侮你啦，……快告訴媽。

芬：（大哭，投入母懷）媽，……我……沒臉再去學校上課了！……我……想死了算了！……

母：德芬，究竟發生了什麼事，你告訴媽，……媽來給你想辦法解決。

芬：媽，……這不是你能解決的問題，……（自書包拿出那份晚報）你有沒有看到今天這份晚報！……我真沒有想到我一向敬愛的父親桑炳成，……原來是個販賣軍火，走私毒品進口的不法商人，同學們都拿著報紙，來問我，是不是眞的？……媽，一個上午，……我都被他們問得快要發瘋了！……

母：（哭著）孩子，……你要媽，怎麼和你說呢，……這是你爸做的好事，……你去問他，……讓他自己來回答你吧！……

（芬走向父的遺像）

芬：（上前跪下）爸，……你究竟是怎樣的一個人？……是大慈善家？還是個僞君子！……爸，……

你怎麼不說話呢！……「罪惡」不是可以用「捐獻」來洗刷乾淨的，……爸，……「名譽」也不是可用「金錢」來購買裝飾的。……這些道理，……你都不知道嗎？……爸！……你留給我們的，不是「榮譽」，是「恥辱」。永遠洗不清的「恥辱」！……我恨你，……（大聲地）恨你……竟然是我的父親！

母：阿香，……快扶小姐去房裡休息，……她的情緒很激動，……別舊病復發了。

香：是，太太。（扶德芬進她自己臥室，下）

母：（不久電話鈴響，母正在發呆，……鈴響了很久，她才如夢初醒似的，去接聽）喂，……我是董事長太太，……你是那一位？是公司的丁秘書，……有什麼事嗎？……你說什麼？……公司的總經理和會計主任串通好，一起拐款潛逃走了！……現在公司亂成一團，副總經理，準備開緊急會議，請大少爺，馬上來一下。（神情木然）啊！……（掛上電話）……德正……

正：德正，……公司出了事，……要你馬上來一下。……你快出來一下。……

母：（聞聲自內出，全身在發抖）媽，……我……快不行了……

正：（慌亂的）德正，……你怎麼啦？……臉發白，……話都說不清楚了！要不要老黃送你去醫院？

母：……老黃，……老黃……

正：（斷斷續續的）媽，……有件事，……我一直瞞著你，……不敢讓你知道，……我……這輩子，……已經……沒有時間，來孝順你了，……我很對不起你。……

七五

母：德正，……你好好的怎麼跟媽媽說這樣的話，……究竟是什麼事？瞞著我不想讓我知道，你快說呀

！……公司等著你去開緊急會議呢！……

正：媽，……我得了「愛滋病」，……醫生說，已經是末期，……沒有救了！……

母：什麼？德正，……你得了「愛滋病」，已經是末期，沒有救了？（音效加強升起）

黃：（正在門口出現）什麼？少爺得了「愛滋病」！

（德正站立不住，倒了下去）

（燈黑、暗轉）

（第三場）

（燈再亮時，僅聚光燈，照在桑炳成的遺像上，母一個人面對遺像，坐在搖椅裡黯然無言，……

四週有乾冰升起，十分悽涼）

（老黃默默的進來，……向董事長遺像行了個禮，再走向太太）

黃：太太，……我也要走了，……

母：謝謝你，……老黃，我也沒法再留你了。……真沒有想到，自從飛機失事以後，一切全變了。……

（黃黯然離去）

母：（走向炳成遺像，用心聲Ｏ・Ｓ，播出母內心的獨白）炳成，……你知道嗎？……你走了以後，
…………

公司出了事，你所有的財產，也都被查封了！……你給我留下的兩個兒子，……大的得了「愛滋病」，……現在住在臺大醫院裡，已奄奄一息！……小的吸毒不說，……最近居然和同學合夥「販賣嗎啡」，已被警察抓到，關進了監獄，不知道，會坐幾年牢，……現在，……老劉，老黃，……他們都走了，只剩阿香還陪在我身邊，……炳成，……這都是你做的「好事」，才讓我活在……這世界上，……就如同活在地獄裡一樣！……

母：（這時，母鳴咽哭泣了起來，……）

（忽一陣陰風吹來，突然，空氣中出現父的聲音）

父：（O‧S）太太，……我錯了，……我對不起你，……你能原諒我嗎？……

母：（訝異的，四週張望著）炳成，……是你在和我說話嗎？……你……在那裡？……你……飛機失事，並沒有死？……

父：（O‧S）我死了，……你真的沒有死？……

母：（駭然，上前）炳成，……你真的沒有死？……

父：（幽然地）不，……我死了，……現在，是我的靈魂，回來看你，……我沒想到，所有的秘密，都曝光了！……

（大門「依呀一聲」開了，一陣輕煙進來，父穿黑色的長袍，像幽靈似的出現在臺上）

母：你忘了，古人說的話嗎？……「若要人不知，除非己莫為」，……做好事，要真的做好事，……像你這樣，假冒爲善，……用做好事，來贖罪，……那是行不通的！……

父：現在我才明白，……可是已經遲了，……來不及了！……我真「後悔」！……

母：你現在「後悔」了，……那有什麼用呢？……什麼用呢？……

（父已在舞臺上消失，母似瘋了的叫著）

母：炳成，……你話還沒說完，……怎麼走了呢？……

（阿香自外進入）

香：太太，天都黑了，你怎麼不開燈呢？……（開燈後客廳大亮）

母：阿香，……老爺，他剛才回來了！……他和我說了不少的話，……

香：太太，……你一定精神錯亂了，……老爺，不是已經死了嗎？……

母：他是死了，……可是……他真的剛才回來過？……

（門鈴響，阿香去開門，不久引項必均自外進入）

項：桑太太，……你還記得我嗎？

母：你是誰？……我不認識你，……是找我捐錢的嗎？……

項：我是項……（依然口吃）……是項……項……必均，……是「人人保險公司」的業務員，……

母：啊，我想起來了，……你是「橡皮筋」，……

打開皮包取出文件及支票）

項：不是……「橡皮筋」，……是項……必均，……桑董事長生前，在我們保險公司，投保了一千萬

的旅行平安保險，……這一次，他意外遭難，公司調查……屬實，……按照保險合約的規定，你是他的合法受益人，……所以公司特地要我把一千萬的支票，親自送到你的手上，……你只要在這上面簽個名，……我就可以把這支票交給你。

母：是嗎？……（看支票）我還有這意外的一千萬，……（看遺像）炳成，……是你派他來給我的？

香：……

香：太太，你快簽字吧，……這可真是「意外」，……

（母簽字收下支票）

項：好了，我……走了，……桑太太，……你以後要出門投保旅行保險，可以找我，……這是我的名片！……（取出名片交母）

母：謝謝你，項先生，再見。……

（項出，母看著支票）

香：太太，明天起，我也要走了。……

母：阿香，你不肯留下來陪陪我嗎？……阿香，你不能走啊！再說，小姐又不肯去上學，終日在房裡哭哭啼啼的，也不能沒有你啊！

（此時，德芬房中，突傳出一聲鎗聲）

母：啊，誰在開鎗？……好像是德芬房裡傳出來的，你快去看看，究竟是怎麼回事？

七九

香：太太，……我去看。（先衝下德芬房，自德芬房中，大聲叫著）小姐，你怎麼開鎗自殺了呢！

母：（在臺上呆住了）德芬，……（大哭起來）德芬，……爲什麼要自殺呢？一定是用德正買回來的那把手鎗，……炳成，……這難道，……是你故意這樣安排的嗎？……炳成，……炳成，……你說話啊！（頹然的昏了過去，倒在臺上。）

幕徐徐下。

—— 劇終

本劇脫稿於民國八十年十月廿九日燈下。

八十一年六月十五日修正。

# 姜龍昭舞臺劇劇本

復　　　活（獨幕劇）三十八年演出。

寶　島　之　蠱（獨幕劇）三十九年演出。

視　　察　　員（獨幕劇）三十九年獲中華文藝獎金委員會獎金並演出。

烽　火　戀　歌（歌舞劇）四十一年由總政治部出版。

榕樹下的黃昏（兒童劇）四十一年獲臺灣省教育廳徵求兒童劇首獎。

奔　向　自　由（獨幕劇）四十二年獲總政治部軍中文藝獎獎第三名，並由總政戰部出版。

國　軍　進　行　曲（五幕劇）四十三年獲總政治部軍中文藝獎多幕劇佳作獎。

父　　與　　子（獨幕劇）五十六年獲「伯康戲劇獎」獨幕劇第四名，並由僑聯出版社出版。

孤　　星　　淚（四幕劇）五十七年獲「伯康戲劇獎」多幕劇首獎，並由僑聯出版社出版。「多少思念多少淚」由遠大文化出版公司出版。曾由中央電影公司改編為「長情萬縷」拍成電影。

紅　　寶　　石（獨幕劇）六十年中國戲劇藝術中心出版。

眼　（四幕劇）六十四年獲「李聖質戲劇獎」首獎，並由商務印書館出版。

八一

吐魯番風雲（五幕劇）六十五年獲「臺北市話劇學會」第三屆藝光獎，並由商務印書館出版。

金蘋果（兒童劇）六十七年獲教育部徵求兒童劇首獎，並由中國戲劇藝術中心出版。

國魂（五幕劇）七十年獲教育部徵求舞臺劇首獎，七十一年又獲總政治作戰部頒發「光華獎」，由遠大文化公司出版。

沒有舌頭的女人（四幕劇）七十一年由遠大文化公司出版。

金色的陽光（四幕劇）七十二年獲行政院文建會徵求舞臺劇首獎，七十三年並由文建會出版。

幾番漣漪幾番情（三幕劇）七十二年受文建會邀請與蔣子安、依風露二人聯合編寫，七十三年由文建會出版。

涙水的沉思（四幕劇）七十四年完成，七十七年定稿，獲教育部徵求舞臺劇文藝創作獎佳作，並由教育部出版。

母親的淚（五幕劇）七十三年獲教育部徵求舞臺劇本文藝創作獎第三名，並由教育部出版。

孟母教子（四幕劇）七十三年完成，七十七年二次修正。

一隻古瓶（四幕劇）七十三年由「文學思潮」雜誌社出版。

陶匠與泥土（四幕劇）七十八年完成。

殘花悲夢（三幕劇）七十九年完成。

飛機失事以後（三幕劇）八十年完成。八十一年由文史哲出版社出版英譯單行本。

About the translator:

Elizabeth Chiang Moxon was born in Mainland China and raised in Taiwan. With a childhood in the Southern Taiwan countryside, she speaks fluent Taiwanese and has warm memories of her early childhood in the country. In 1961, she was chosen by the Japanese NIKAZU Film Company through a join venture with the Chinese government. She received basic training in film making and acting at the studio in the outskirts of Tokyo. Three months later, upon her return from Japan, she was under contract as an actress for The Central Motion Picture Theater Company.

She continued her high school, and subsequently college. Within the two years after she returned from Japan, other than attending school, she spent all her time in theater related work. It included: One talk show " The Golden Age", a comedy series " Three young Phoenix", two movies, two stage shows, and a half dozen television theaters. All of her television shows were produced by Taiwan Television Co. then the only network in the country. In 1964, she joined The Civil Air Transport Air Line as a stewardess; she also did a great deal of advertising for them.

She was married in 1967 to John Moxon, a U.S. Navy officer who was the Aide to the Joint Chief of Taiwan Defense Commander. In 1968, while her husband started work for Morgan Guaranty Trust Co. of New York, she studied at The Packer Collegiate Institute. Later she got a B.A. in American Studies from Douglass College, Rutgers University. Elizabeth has devoted her entire life to raising their four children and doing volunteer work for the community and schools.

Now that the children are older, she is back in her theater related work again. In 1991, she translated her first play " Tears in Silence" and although not up to her standards, it roused her desire to improve. In October 1991, she returned to Taiwan and appeared in a stage play "An Antique Vase", her first play in twenty-eight years. In 1992, she worked on a new play "After The Plane Crash". She finished it on the fifteenth anniversary of her mother's death in honor of her mother.

# AFTER THE PLANE CRASH

An Original Play

by

Chiang Lung Chao

Translated into English

by

Elizabeth Chiang Moxon

John Sawyer Moxon, Editor

Jun 1992

The Liberal Arts Press
P. O. Box 7-99, TAIPEI, TAIWAN
REPUBLIC OF CHINA
1992

**Time**:   Now, or another time that is applicable.

**Act One**:          A September afternoon.

**Act Two**:          Three days after Act one.

**Act Three**:        Scene one:  A month later, in October, about 7 p.m.

                    Scene two:  A week later.

                    Scene three:  Five days later.

**Place**:   Taipei, or a similar city.

**Scenery**:  All three Acts take place in the Sanders' living room.

> Stage design is based on a well to do businessman's home.
> There are stairs which go up to the master bedroom.  The main
> stage consists of a door which leads to an outside main gate,
> doors to the dining room, kitchen, and  three bedrooms for two
> men and one woman.  Next to the living room is a study with a
> desk, a safe, a sofa or love seat; there is light switch that the
> audience can see the motion of which from the study.   The
> center stage is the formal living room.  It consists of a sofa,
> telephone, rocking chair, and any necessities to make it look
> elegant and luxurious.   An important detail is a large board
> hanging on the wall, that states "KINDNESS AND CHARITY".

The third scene is after the plane crash.  The living room has an altar
     with flowers, fruit, and incense burner.  A large picture of Ben
     hangs above the altar.

**Characters**:

**Ben**: A successful businessman in his fifties.

**Sandy**: Ben's wife, in her fifties, well dressed, kind and gentle.

**Ted**: Ben's oldest son, in his twenties, a playboy type.

**Fay**: Ben's only daughter, about twenty, a college student.  Nice but
     naive, with a pleasant personality.  After the kidnapping, she
     has a nervous breakdown.  A tragic figure.

1

**Sam**: Ben's second son, in high school, about 18, a drug addict.

**Datsun**: Ben's nephew, works for Ben, stationed in Los Angeles, California, U.S. in his early thirties.

**Mary**: Ben's cousin, in her forties, modern dresser. She is a busybody, full of tricks and ideas, quite ambitious.

**Mr. Young**: Head of an orphanage, a humble and kind person.

**Shane**: A cute and funny young maid, in her twenties. (or a middle aged woman) (whatever the director desires)

**Juan**: Ben's chauffeur, a middle aged loyal worker.

**Robert Bond**: An insurance salesman, stutters when nervous or embarrassed.

# Act 1

**Time**: A September afternoon.

**Scenery**: The living room of the Sanders.

**Characters**: Shane, Robert Bond, Mr.Young. Ben, Sandy, Ted, Sam, Fay,
Datsun, Mary.

> When the curtain goes up, Shane is working in the living room, cleaning, either humming or with some music in the background. The door bell rings, Shane stops,goes out and brings Robert in. Robert looks around, impressed by the surroundings, while Shane goes to pour him a cup of tea.

Shane: Sir, please have some tea. What is your name? You are here for Mr. Sanders ?

Robert: Yes, miss, my name is Robert Bond. I am here to .........

Shane: What? Your name is rubber Bond? Are you serious....?

Robert: No, I am Robert Bond, the Bond that is the same as James Bond. This is my name card. (hands his business card to her)

Shane: Oh, I see, for a moment I thought someone was trying to play a joke on me, or a joke on your life, for that matter. Well, what can I do for you?

Robert: I am the salesman for "Gem Gem Insurance Co." I am here to sell insurance, either life or property........It is beneficial to have insurance.

Shane: Bologna, you are full of trash!

Robert: (shocked,embarrassed and starts to stutter) Miss, you........,why.........why....are you talking like this? I......I.....I have never......done..... done anything to you.....why.....why you .....you....you.......

3

Shane: Me, what?

Robert: Why are you so hostile?.......We...we are doing it for people's own protection.

Shane: That is why I said that your insurance company and your sales agents are full of Bologna. I have learned my lessons from you people. A few years ago we bought some insurance for my mother. After she died, the insurance company wouldn't pay. They claimed that my mother didn't declare that she had a heart problem. How would we know what she had, we are not doctors. If we all have to be healthy, and live forever, why would we need you? The worst part of it is that they wouldn't even give back the money we had paid. My father was so mad he almost had a stroke over it. You blood suckers!

Robert: Miss, our Company is different, we are partners with an American insurance company, we are world wide, international. We are legitimate, we guarantee that we.........we....

Shane: Yeah, I know that you guarantee that you....you.....you.....you will not pay!

Robert: Miss.......you....you listen to me, do...do...do I look like a bad person?....... do....do I look like......I cheat people?

Shane: Well, let me see....

Robert: Can't you tell?

Shane: No, of course I can't tell. There is no brand on your face to indicate that you are a good or bad person. That is precisely the problem; people can't tell the good from the evil. Some people look and act like angels; actually they are devils in disguise. How can I tell? That is why I don't trust you at all. I think you'd better leave now, I don't think we want to buy any insurance from you.

Robert: Miss....you...you......please don't do this, I'll leave as soon as I talk to your master first.

Shane: You told me that you came to see my master; if I knew that you were selling insurance, I would never have let you in. Gees,

4

now I see that you are more like chewing gum than a rubber band, I can't even get rid of you.

Robert: Miss, please, I am Robert Bond, don't make fun of me........

(In the meantime, Sandy the Mistress comes down the stairs)

Sandy: Shane, who are you talking to? You are making such a racket.

Shane: I am talking to an insurance salesman, someone named rubber bend.

Robert: (walking toward Sandy) Good afternoon ma'am, my name is Robert Bond, this is my name card, I am working for the Gem Gem Insurance Company.

Sandy: (takes his card,takes a glance at it) Oh, Mr. Bond, I am very sorry; we have plenty of insurance already, and we don't need any more.

Robert: Yes,ma'am. This is my first experience as salesman, I.......I am not too good with words........I have some pamphlets here for you to look at, in case you are interested, please feel free to call me.

Sandy: (Takes the papers) Sure, in the future, if I need any, I'll call you.

Robert: Thank you ma'am. (leaves, when near the door, turns around adding) Don't.......don't.......don't forget to call, please.

Shane: We know, we know. ( waves her hand to signal him out and closes the door behind him)

Sandy: Shane, from now on, don't let anybody in, unless it is someone who we know or are expecting. Now-a-days you have to be careful; there are too many crazy and evil people around.

Shane: Yes, ma'am.

(Fay comes out of her room with a nice dress and a few books in her arm)

Fay: Hi, Mom, do you like this?

5

Sandy: Oh, that's nice, you look so beautiful in it. Fay, you are getting prettier by the day, I am so proud!

Fay: Don't I look just like you, when you were my age?

Sandy: (laughs and gives her a hug) Look at you, you even know how to flatter your own mother. You still have classes this afternoon?

Fay: Yeah, Sociology, it is a required course.

Sandy: Keep up your good work, dear. After you graduate from college, I'll send you to the United States to do post graduate work. Mom is so proud of you!

Fay: Really? That is great!

Sandy: Of course, I never kid around about your future. Fay, your brothers, they never were good students like you are, when I think of them, I always feel a bit of disappointment.

Fay: Mom, stop that. Even though Ted dropped out of college, now he is working for Dad, that's not so bad.

Sandy: That is because he is your father's son, if it were someone else, he would have been fired a long time ago. You can never find him in the office; all his friends are useless losers. Liquor and women, darn it , I don't know how he is going to handle the responsibility of the company in the future.

Fay: Mom, in that case, you and Dad better teach him or figure out some way to get him straightened out.

Sandy: I know. Your father is so busy, he doesn't have time to look over Ted's shoulder all the time. What I say doesn't seem help much either.

Fay: Mom, don't worry too much. It will all be fine. By the way, I just joined a community service group. we are doing a fund raising to get money to develop some projects to serve the needs of the aborigines. I need to contribute.

Sandy: How much do you have in mind?

Fay: How about one hundred thousand?

Sandy: Fay, I don't mind if you give a little more than the others. but a hundred thousand for your age, isn't that a bit too much showing off, don't you think?

Fay: Mom, I want to be the leader, I should set a good example. Come on, be generous, when you give to charities yourself, it always half a million or more.Please, pretty please......

Sandy: All right! Whatever you say, you know me, as long as it will truly help others, I don't mind. However, young lady, you are still in school, the academics are still the most important thing. I want you to focus more on your studies, rather than on your extra curricular activities. Do you hear? I will be supportive if you keep up with your grades, do we have a deal?

Fay: Yes, I know and don't worry.

Sandy: Wonderful,I know that I always can count on my sweet girl. (mother embraces daughter joyfully)

(Ben comes down the stairs,finishing buttoning his shirt and fixing his tie)

Sandy: How come you are down? Don't you want to rest a bit more?

Ben: I can't. The head of "ANGEL ORPHANAGE" Mr. Young is coming to see me. After that I have to stop by at the office any way. Fay, come here, let me take a good look at you; it has been a while since I gave you a hug.

Fay: You are so right, Dad. You have been very busy, look at you, I think you have lost some weight. (Fay hugs, kisses,and holds her father. Sandy quietly leaves them alone)

Ben: Really? You think so?

Fay: Yes, Dad, you ought to take better care of yourself. As the famous saying goes, " Even if you owned the whole world, if you lost your health, what good does it do for you?" Do you agree, Dad?

Ben: (Smiling) My sweet daughter, all of a sudden you are so grown up, even trying to lecture your old man. Of course I agree with you! Do you remember, it seems not that long ago when I held your hand to cross the street for a hot dog. All of a sudden you are a college student and want to take care of your old papa now. My, time sure goes by fast .

Fay: Dad, a long time ago, you told me that you were going to give a big party for my twentieth birthday, do you still remember?

Ben: Of course I remember, how could I forget my promise for such a big event in our lives. Not only that , I also told you that I'd buy you a big diamond ring, so that you can show off on your wedding day. Am I right?

Fay: Stop that, Dad. I am still young, I don't want to get married yet, not for a long long time.

Ben: Oh, yeah? Tell me, do you have any boy that you like? If you do, you ought to bring him home for us to meet.

Fay: No, Dad, I don't have any boyfriend yet. Believe me, if I have one, I definitely will let you check him out first.

Ben: Good, make sure that you keep your promise. Sweetie.

(Sandy comes downstairs holding a jacket)

Sandy: Don't forget your jacket, it is getting chilly, you don't want to come down with a cold. (she helps Ben to put it on)

Fay: (Takes a look at her watch) Mom, I better go, and please don't forget my donation money. When will you have it?

Sandy: Tomorrow, I don't have that much cash now.

Ben: What money?

Sandy: Fay's school has a fund raising. She asked me to give a hundred thousand, I said that I'd do it.

Ben: What kind of fund raising? for what group?

8

Fay: It's a community service project, It is a social service for the needy aborigines.

Ben: It sounds to me like it is for a good cause. A hundred thousand might not be enough, why don't we give more, how about two hundred thousand? I'll write you a check to take with you, allright?

Fay: (gives Ben a big hug and kiss) Oh, Dad, you are wonderful, you are the best, I am so proud of you!

(Ben writes a check and hands it over to Fay)

Fay: Thank you Dad, goodbye Mom, I am on my way.

Sandy: Fay, don't stay out too late, make sure you don't take a cab or do anything alone. You can't be careful enough, do you hear? Last night Shane ran into someone who exposed himself and scared the daylights out of her. Please be careful!

Fay: Yes, Mom, I'll be careful.

Ben: Fay, there are too many nuts around, we love you so much, we wouldn't know what to do if anything happened to you, do you understand?

Fay: Yes, Dad. I am not a baby any more, I'll take good care of myself. I better get going, see you all later, bye. (Fay opens the door and exits off stage)

Ben: Where are our two sons? either of them home?

Sandy: Ted is out, apparently one of his old buddies came home from abroad, I am sure he should be home soon.

Ben: Where is the little one then? Didn't we get a notification that he had cut too many classes in school? Can't you get some control or discipline over him?

Sandy: At his age, what can I do? Let me check, may be he is sleeping up in his room. ( She goes to one of the rooms and comes right back)

Ben: Well? not there?

Sandy: No, he probably went to the video arcade again. That kid, he is hooked on those games. God knows how many times I have talked to him, it is like talking to a mirror.......

Ben: No wonder those Video Arcades sprang up like mushrooms. It is so easy to make money out of those kids.

(Door bell rings, Shane opens the door and brings Mr. Young in)

Shane: Mr. Young is here ma'am.

Sandy: How are you Mr. Young? We have been waiting for you, please sit down. Shane, please bring Mr. Young some tea.

Ben: (Gets a check out of his pocket, shakes Mr.Young's hand first then hands over a check)  This is a cashier's check, you may cash it any time.

Young: (With a look of surprise)  A million, oh, dear, you're contributing a million?

Ben: Mr.Young, you have contributed your whole life to the orphanage; this is the least that I can do. You have so many kids over there, a small amount is not going to help much to offset the rise in prices.

Young: Mr.Sanders, I don't know how to thank you. Truly,I am surprised. Although there are many wealthy people around, they are not nearly so charitable as you are. You've made my day. I am  representing our kids to thank you for your generosity. For the last few years, if it weren't for you, we couldn't have done as much for our kids. I don't know what to say to show you our appreciation.........

Ben: Stop, don't say any more, it gives me pleasure to do it . You know the saying that it is more blessed to give than to receive.

Young: Bless your heart. The way you help your fellow people, I am sure the Lord will bring you happiness and fulfillment (gets out a receipt book to write the receipt)

Ben: Thank you, if there is anything at all that I can do or help with in the future please feel free to call, I'll do my best .

Sandy: We mean it, sometimes when Ben is too busy,I'll help, just give me a call. We both feel strongly about charitable work. we'll support you all the way.

Young: Thank you both so much, here is the receipt. When you have a chance, we would love to have you come and visit with our kids.

Ben: Yes, definitely we will, I am sure Sandy will go soon as she has a chance and bring plenty of candy for the kids.

Young: That would be great, I better get going now, thank you again.

Ben: Do you want my driver to give you a lift?

Young: Oh, no, thank you. I am o.k. goodbye.

(Phone ring, Sandy picks up the phone)

Sandy: Yes, you are at the airport? great, here he is. (Hands the phone to Ben) It is your nephew Datsun.

Ben: Yes, so good to hear your voice, ................good, I'll be here, we'll discuss more when you are here. (hangs up the phone)

Sandy: Ben, what kind of business is Datsun handling for you in L.A.? You two act like there is some big secret, what's going on?

Ben: Stop nagging, so long as it is not a mistress, why should you worry about it? Trust me, do I look like some one who will ever do anything wrong? You never were interested in my Trading business, what's the matter with you now?

Sandy: The more you want to hide from me, the more I get curious, what is it, come on, I must find out now.

Ben: All right, let me tell you, it is antiques, Chinese antiques. There are
Porcelains, bronze, and artifacts. We could make a lot of money on this deal.

Sandy: Fine, you see, now you explained and made it clear. I don't worry about it any more, simple, it is merely communication .

11

Ben: (Looks at his watch) Dear, I've got to go to the office for a while, I'll
    be home soon. When Datsun gets here, ask him to stay for
    dinner and make sure we have some good dishes for our
    celebration.

Sandy: Yes dear, I'll take care of it.

Ben: Shane, ask Juan to get the car ready, I am on my way to office.

Shane: Juan has been waiting, sir..

(Ben picks up his hat and jacket or coat and walks out the door)

Sandy: Shane, go to the kitchen and tell Leo that our nephew is
    coming for dinner, I want an extra fancy menu for tonight.

Shane: Yes, Ma'am. (goes off to the back)

Sandy: It's strange that I have'nt seen Ted or Sam today, I hope
    nothing bad has happened.

(door bell rings)

Sandy: Shane, go get the door, it's probably Ted.

(Shane goes to the door and brings in a well dressed middle aged
    woman with a loud and clear voice)

Mary: How are you Sandy, is Ben home?

Sandy: I am fine, thank you. I am sorry, you just missed him. Sit down
    please. Can I offer you something to drink?

Mary: Thank you, may I have a cup of mocha please.

Shane: Yes, Ma'am, I'll be right back.

Sandy: I have not seen you for a long time, where have you been?
    What have you been doing?

Mary: Well, I just got back from a trip to South Asia. I am exhausted,
    after all that travel, I still find my home here is the best place to

live. How about you? Sandy, what have you been doing? Why don't you travel around a bit with that dear cousin of mine?

Sandy: Well, I am kind of lazy, and your cousin Ben is so wrapped up in his business, he doesn't even have time of his own. I wouldn't even think about travel or vacation. It has been a while since I saw you last. What are you up to?

Mary: I am in kind of a jam. I want to talk to Ben to see whether he could help me out.

Sandy: Ben just left for the office; you missed him by two minutes. You can tell me just the same. If there is any thing that we can do, you know that we'll try our best.

(Shane brings in the coffee, serves and leaves)

Mary: (has a sip of her coffee) Well, I have a relative who got into a business deal to bring in a shipment of medicinal herbs. However the shipment was seized by the customs officials and now has been impounded by the government.

Sandy: You mean they were smuggled in?

Mary: Sort of, they asked a fishing boat to do the transporting. The cargo was precious herbs, there were ginseng, deer hoofs........ worth five or six million dollars.

Sandy: Gee, that is a shame.

Mary: Exactly, it will be such a waste, if it gets confiscated permanently. That is why I am here to ask whether Ben knows anybody who can help us out. We'd be happy to pay the penalty, if we could get our cargo back.

Sandy: Well, this is hard.

Mary: We'd be happy to pay the person for the favor.

Sandy: Mary, I am pretty sure that Ben will not want to have anything to do with this.

Mary: Ben always helps people out, why can't he help his own family?

13

Sandy: Your cousin Ben will do anything for charities, community services, but when it comes to smuggling, illegal shady deals, he will not have anything to do with it. He always stresses the importance of honesty and integrity. I don't think he will be able to help your friend at all.

Mary: I know all that and I agree with you. But this relative of mine said that if he looses this cargo, it will be the end of the world for him, he is likely to kill himself........

Sandy: Really? Are you serious?

Mary: If it were not the case, I wouldn't even be here. The money he used to buy the goods was borrowed from a loan shark. If anything goes wrong, he is dead one way or another. You must help him, to save a life, please.

Sandy: It is not that I don't want to help, it is your cousin, you know how stubborn he is. He is always preaching against things like this, how can I persuade him to change what he stands for?

Mary: You are his wife, can't you tell him that it is for your relative?

Shandy: I have run into his brick wall temperament before, he is so stubborn, that I couldn't get any where. If you want to give a try, wait until he comes home. You talk to him yourself, see what he says. Actually he does know quite a few people at customs. After all, the smuggled goods are only herbs, they are not the harmful stuff like drugs or arms. You never know, he might just do it for you.

Mary: Do you think that he is still in his office now?

Sandy: I think so, he said that he'd be back soon for dinner. Relax, you stay put and wait for him. I would love to have you join us for dinner.

Mary: Never mind dinner, people are waiting for me to get back to them.

Sandy: In that case, I 'll call and ask him to come home right now.

(Sandy picks up the phone and dials) Hello, Tina, may I speak to Ben please?.....he left ? when?.... alright, that's great, you have a

14

nice day. thank you. (hangs up the phone and says to Mary)
Ben already left the office and is on his way home. Don't worry,
you two will figure out some way.

Mary: Great, then I'll wait.

Sandy: Tell me, did you have money in this deal too?

Mary: Yes, other wise I wouldn't bother you and Ben.

(Door bell rings, Shane gets the door, Ted comes in with his arm in a
sling and a bandaged forehead)

Sandy: Maybe Ben is home. (turns around and sees Ted, shocked)
What happened to you? My goodness, look at you. Who did
this to you? I thought you went to a luncheon, not a battle field.

Mary: Ted, are you O.K? Were you in a car accident?

Ted: Hi Mom, Aunt Mary, I am O.K. Don't worry,this is only a surface
wound. The Doctor checked and it's no big deal, it will be fine
in a few days.

Sandy: What has happened? Were you in a fight?

Mary: Come on, young man, tell us, what was it?

Ted: We started out to have lunch in a restaurant, we had a bit to drink,
then we moved our party to a bar. At the bar, we ran into some
jerks. We got into a disagreement, a fistfight started and,
wouldn't you know it, one of them got a gun out and started
shooting. Fortunately the police got there in time and no one
was seriously hurt.

Sandy: Just listening to you scares me to death, what if a bullet had hit
you, this is life and death, do you understand?

Ted: Don't worry, Mom, they were just showing off, trying to scare us,
no big deal.

Mary: For goodness sake, from now on you better stay away from
those dangerous places.

Ted: Aunt Mary, I am not a kid any more, I have been around, I am not afraid.

Sandy: Ted, I am warning you, if you ever get yourself into fights or any dangerous situations like that again, you better not come home to face me.

Ted: Mom, you don't know, now-a-days if you are not aggressive enough, people will think that you are a wimp and take advantage of you. You have to show them how strong you are, in order to stand on your own.................

(Door bell rings, Shane opens the door and Ben walks in, takes off his hat. Ted sees his father and tries to avoid him by leaving the stage and walking into his room, but Ben has seen him)

Mary: How are you Ben?

Ben: Good to see you Mary. What can I do for you? I know you wouldn't be here, unless there is something. What is it?

Mary: Yes, Ben, you are right. I need a favor from you. A friend of mine got into a business deal. He imported a shipment of medicinal herbs; however, the customs officials seized the boat and confiscated the cargo. I know you have a lot of contacts in the customs office; I wonder whether you can help me to make a deal to just pay the penalty and get the cargo back.

Ben: It sounds like your friend is in the smuggling business, right?

Mary: Kind of, but........

Ben: Say no more, this kind of thing has happened quite often lately. I think it is terrible, I am sorry that I am not able to help you.

Mary: Ben, this shipment is worth a few million dollars, I have a share in it too. Because of me, you have to help, we are willing to pay a handsome sum to smooth things over.

Ben: You are asking me to help you in something that is illegal. That is out of the question, no, I am sorry.

Mary: (using a soft voice) Dear cousin Ben, are you going to watch me sink and drown?

Ben: Stop it Mary, how can you talk like this? It is not that I won't help, I have my own integrity and principles. If I help you with illegal matters, how could I ever conduct business with an honest reputation? Don't you realize the consequences?

Mary: O.K. Stop, I know. I am sorry to have bothered you, I better go now.

Sandy: Mary, come on, don't be upset. Why don't you stay for dinner, we'll talk, .........for me, please.

Mary: No thank you, Sandy, I couldn't eat anything now anyway.

Ben: Mary, how much did you have in this deal? Let me help you out.

Mary: No, thank you, I am o.k. I am leaving. (Mary walks out)

Sandy: Ben, you have hurt your cousin's feeling .

Ben: There is nothing that I can do.

Sandy: (sigh) trouble, trouble..........

Ben: By the way, where is Ted? I did see him with bandage on his head and arm in a sling, didn't I. Did he get into another fight?

Sandy: Well....it is not too bad. The Doctor said in a few days he will be fine.

Ben: Tell him to come out, I want to talk to him.

Sandy: (Walks toward Ted's room and calls out) Ted, please come out for a minute, your father wants to talk to you.

Ted: (Comes out of his room, sheepishly) Yes, Dad.

Ben: How bad is your wound?

Ted: Not too bad, Dad, the Doctor said that in a couple of days I will be fine.

Ben: Good, in that case, you have no problem going to work on Monday then.

Ted: Yes, I think I will be fine by then.

Ben: You are twenty-five years old . You should be mature and independent by now. How can you still act like a juvenile delinquent? When I was your age, I was on my own and responsible enough to earn a living. You wanted to drop out of college, I didn't force you to stay; I figured you might learn your trade on the job. I have always hoped that if you could diligently learn the business, I could hand it over to you.......

Ted: I know, Dad.

Ben: If you know, why do you still act so immature? You never stay long enough in your office for anybody to find you. Instead, you hang around bars, women, and the casinos. You think I don't know what is going on; actually I have you under surveillance. I have to check on the behavior of my future executives; it is company policy; don't you know that?

Ted: Yes, Dad, I will try to do better.

Ben: Please try hard. Next month, I'm taking a trip to Thailand; It will take about a month to wrap up the whole thing.

Sandy: A trip to Thailand? What's it all about? Is it business?

Ben: Of course it is business related. I plan to open a couple of branch offices there. I also would like to pay a visit to my old friends.

Ted: Dad, may I go with you?

Ben: No, for the time being, that is not necessary. Actually what I have in mind is to put you in charge of the sales department. If you do a good job while I am away, then I will promote you to vice president and gradually let you take over the Company. If you can't handle it, then I am sorry but I will just have to hire an outsider to run the business eventually. Do I make myself clear to you? Do you understand the out come of this?

Ted: Very clear, Dad.

Ben: After I leave, while you are in charge, there are some important things that I want you to accomplish for me.

Ted: What are they?

Sandy: (Gratefully) You two talk, I'll go to check the dinner.

Ben: You do that, and I will talk to you about my trip latter.

(Sandy walks off to the kitchen)

Ben: I want you to run a check on all the top executives. I want to know their productivity, working habits, loyalty and even their private lives and personal affairs. I want to know exactly what they do every waking moment. I want a complete documented report on them. Do you think you can manage all these?

Ted: Dad, I will try my best.

Ben: I ask you to check on them. At the same time, I have someone checking on you too. They are going to give me a report on you also.

Ted: Dad, You are sharp and devious.

Ben: To run a business successfully is to know how to delegate qualified personnel. However, to know who to trust is the hardest. People knows how to pretend and cheat. A person quite often has multiple faces. You rarely can tell the good from the evil easily. The real personality is hard to reveal, you know like the Dr. Jekyl and Mr. Hyde. The old saying states: " The hardest thing is to be a well liked person, but it is even harder to know a person truly well" In order to protect my business, I have to do what is necessary. Now you just started in business, You must learn and don't forget what I told you.

Ted: Yes, Dad. I will remember.
(door bell rings, Shane opens and brings Datsun in)

Shane: Sir, your nephew is here.

Datsun: How are you uncle Ben? Gee, what happened to you, Ted?

Ted: Nothing, just got into a fight, no big deal. Did you just arrive today?

Datsun: Yes, straight from the airport.

Ben: You better get some rest, son. I will talk to your cousin for a while.

Ted: Yes, Dad. I'll see you at dinner. (Ted goes to his room )

Ben: How have you been? You look good, how was the flight?

Datsun: Not too bad, I slept a bit on the plane. Hopefully I will not have any jetlag. I am sorry that I am late; the traffic was jammed all the way here.

Ben: Oh, no problem, traffic jams come with "prosperity" and a better life, right? As a matter of fact I just finished a few things myself. Come on, let's talk in my study.

Datsun: Great! (follows Ben to the study, Ben turns on a light, sits down with Datsun who gets out some papers to show to Ben and they get into a serious discussion. The audience can't hear them; later Shane brings tea to them, then backs out, runs into Sandy coming from the kitchen)

Sandy: Shane, did my nephew arrive? (turns on living room light)

Shane: Yes, ma'am. He is in the study talking to Mr.Sanders.

Sandy: Fine, you better go help the cook and set the table. We are going to eat soon.

Shane: Yes, ma'am, right a way.

(Sam quietly comes in from outside, with a book bag)

Sandy: Where have you been Sam, it is way past your school hour.

Sam: (tooking a look at the study carefully) Hey, Mom, is Dad home already?

Sandy: Yes, Your cousin is here too, hurry up, go clean up, we are going to eat dinner soon.

20

Sam: Yes, Mom, but before I go can you give me some money? After dinner I am going out with some friends to buy books.

Sandy: How much do you need?

Sam: Five thousand.

Sandy: What? What happened to the money that I gave you yesterday? You spent it all already?

Sam: I didn't spend it. I lost it at the video arcade, playing Pachinco.

Sandy: For goodness sake, you are too young to gamble, did you learn that in school?

Sam: (Jokingly) Of course not, I learned from my classmates. Please............pretty please. (Reaches his hands out making begging gesture looks kind of cute and naughty)

Sandy: (Reluctantly gives in, gets money and hands it to him) Here you are, take it easy, no more gambling.

Sam: Yes, Mom. You are the best! (puts money in his pocket and walks toward his room)

Sandy: You better hurry, get yourself cleaned up for dinner.

Sam: (Yells back) Yes, Mom.

Sandy: (Walks toward the study) Ben, shall we eat?

Ben: Yes, let's eat now. (both walk out of the study) Datsun, I am going to toast you for doing a wonderful job on this deal. I am so proud of you!

Datsun: Thank you, Uncle Ben. By the way Aunt Sandy, I have a present for you. (gets a bottle of perfume from his brief case and hands it to Sandy) I hope this is your favorite scent.

Sandy: (takes a look at the label) Thank you so much, this is exactly my favorite brand, you were so sweet to remember me. You must be starving and exhausted after the long trip. Let's eat; we can talk while we are eating. (she leads the way toward the dining room)

21

Datsun: (Follows her) Yes, Aunty. (Everyone walks toward the dining room) (Phone rings, Shane gets it and calls out for Ben)

Shane: Sir, telephone for you.

Ben: (picks up the phone, listens) Yes, this is Ben, What did you say? (at the sound of Ben's voice, everyone stops and turns to look at him, the stage sound effects now amplify the threatening voice of the kidnapper)

Kidnapper: Your daughter is in our hands; if you want her back, you better prepare fifty million ransom money in three days. No police authorities, no tricks, if you attempt to try anything, your daughter will be dead. (Fay's voice is heard over the phone, calling for her father to help. The phone clicks.)

Ben: Hellow, hellow........ oh..... my god, they've kidnapped my daughter. (loudly) They got Fay.

Datsun: They got Fay?

Ben: Yes, they want fifty million ransom, and no police.

Sandy: Oh, dear god, my baby. (starts to cry, appears shaky and weak, Datsun reaches out for her) (Ted and Sam rush out of their room)

Ted: Dad, what happened, who got kidnapped?

Sam: Is it Fay? Mom? (Sandy appears to be passing out)

Ben: Dame, how am I going to do it in three days?

Lights out, Curtains down, end of the first act.

22

## Act Two

**Time**: Three days later.

**Scene**: Same as last one.

**Characters**: Same as Act One.

Curtains up, lights on. Ted is reading a newspaper, his arm no longer is in a sling, his forehead still has a bandage. Ben sits right next to the phone with a cigaret, puffing one after another. He looks overly exhausted, painfully stares into the air. the atmosphere is tense. (Phone rings, Ben picks up the phone)

Ben: Hellow, yes, what? Nobody showed up?........... I know it is over an hour............... no, nobody called.......... they didn't change this meeting location yet............. please, Sandy don't cry,.................You just have to be patient and wait there, they will come.........O.K? (Hangs up the phone, holds his face, rubs his head, trying to release his pain)

Ted: Dad, is that Mom?

Ben: Yes, nobody showed up yet, she is beside herself. Dammed, they insist on your mother delivering the money, poor thing. They have changed the location of the drop off point so many times, I don't know what kind of joke they are pulling, your poor mother........

Ted: I still think you should report this to the authorities. If those criminals get away with this, they are going to do it again and again, then there is no peace for anyone.

Ben: I know what you are saying, but when it comes to my daughter, I don't want to run any risk. What if they found out that I went to the police and got mad and kill my daughter. No way, the money does not mean anything to me when it comes to my children's lives.

Ted: I disagree with you, If they get away this time, they might do it again, they figure that you have plenty of money and are willing to give up without a fight, then what are you going to do?

23

Ben: For Christ's sake, are you still arguing with me?

Ted: Dad, I am not arguing with you. I just say how will they know
whether we go to the police or not? At least, if the police work
on it ,we might have a chance to catch them. Now, after they
get the money, if they decide to kill her, there is not a thing that
we can do. I think I better call the police now.

(Ted gets up reaches for the phone, Ben stands up trying to stop him)

Ben: Please, don't, not at this stage. If anything changes they will kill
your sister for sure. If you don't think of me, think of your
mother, do you think she could handle it? (Ben breaks down
crying, Ted holds him and comforts him)

Ted: All right, I won't do it. It's up to you. Somehow I don't think that
we are doing the right thing.

(Door bell rings, Ted goes to open the door and brings Robert Bond in)

Ted: Dad, he said he is looking for you, his last name is Bond.

Ben: Mr. Bond? Do I know you?

Bond: Sir, My name is Robert Bond,( gets out name card hands it to
Ben) I am selling insurance............I have been here before.........
you weren't here.......
I......I....Wonder........whether.....you.......you... want to buy
some more insurance........

Ben: (looking at him with great interest) You are an Insurance
salesman? are you selling door to door?

Robert: Yes, everybody has to make a living....... I..........I thought......I
will give..........a.....a try. Everybody needs some kind of
in........in......

Ben: Insurance, you mean. right?

Robert: Yes, sir. You..... you are so......so ......so right. I am so
sorry......when....I.....I....got nervous.......I.....I s......s.....stutter.

Ben: That's alright, how much do you want me to buy, you tell me. It just happened that I am going on a business trip, do you sell travel insurance?

Robert: Yes......we do have......all kinds of insurance. (Opens his brief case gets out a stack of brochures and hands them to Ben) You..........You can take a look, and decide for yourself.

Ted: Dad, why bother with him, tell him to go.

Ben: You never know what is going to happen tomorrow. As long as I am going to be on the road, why don't I get some.

Robert: Right, sir. You......you....you are so.....so....so smart.

Ben: In that case, I think I'll get a ten million dollar policy.

Robert: (Shocked) Ten....ten.....ten.....mil....lion?

Ben: (Smiling) Yes, ten million. Do I need a physical?

Robert: Yes, you.....you....do need a Phy......phy.....physical, it is...... a.....a.... large policy.

Ben: How much do I have to pay you?

(Robert takes out a calculator to compute, he thinks he has the number, hands it to Ben, then takes it back again. He does this a few times)

Robert: I....am.....so..so.. sorry sir, you are so kind and I am so nervous, I don't seem able to get it right.

Ben: Mr. Bond, don't bother with it now, ( gets out a name card and hands it to him ) Tomorrow you come to my office and talk to my secretary, figure it out. Before I leave, I'll get a physical then we will settle the whole thing. I am busy now anyway. Ted will see you out.

Robert: Yes, sir. that's great, thank you and goodbye.

(Ted sees Robert out)

Ben: (Shakes his head and smiles) I can't believe that he is a salesman, but, you have to give him credit for trying hard to earn a living.

(Ted comes in with Mary)

Ted: Dad, Aunt Mary is here to see you.

Mary: Ben, I was so horrified to hear that Fay was kidnapped. how is everything now? Did you report it to the police?

Ben: No, I didn't report it. They said that if I did, they would kill her. I didn't even negotiate the ransom with them. Sandy is dropping the money off right now. The last three days, they have changed the location so many times, God knows what's the matter with them.

Mary: They might think that you reported it to the police, that's why they wouldn't dare show up.

Ben: I don't know what to think, I hope they didn't kill her.

Mary: No, I wouldn't think so.

Ben: Oh, God, there were some cases that they killed the victim after they got the ransom money. Oh, what have people became, what kind of society is this?

Ted: Dad, calm down. I still think we should report it to the police, at least we would have the authorities on our side.

Ben: No! I can't risk your sister's life, other than reporting it to the police, do you have any better ideas?

Mary: Ben, I have an idea, do you want to hear? Do you remember the other day you turned me down on the smuggled goods case? Another friend of mine introduced us to a politician, just one phone call, the whole thing was settled. Now-a-days money sometimes is not enough. We also need power and prestige.

Ben: Are you telling me that politicians have power in dealing with kidnappers?

Mary: It is hard to say, you never know.

Ted: Dad, why don't you ask Aunt Mary to ask that politician to help.

Ben: Mary, do you think that he would help?

Mary: Well, I don't know. Boy, it is refreshing that you have to ask me for help.

Ben: For Christ sake, at this point, how can you talk like this?

Mary: I am just kidding. O.K. I'll give it a try.

(Phone ring, Ted answers)

Ted: Hello, speaking, oh Lily, I am sorry, I am tied up here, I can't come out tonight. ........Alright, I'll call you in a few days. goodbye.

Ben: Who is it?

Mary: Is it your girlfriend?

Ben: Ted, I don't mind it if you are dating nice girls or have a few good girl friends. You better stay away from those gold diggers and bimbos. They are all up to no good, do you understand?

Ted: Yes, Dad, I will be careful.

Ben: Mary, seriously, do you really think that politician friend of yours can help?

Mary: He has a reputation for getting things done. Regardless what kind of people, shady or not, he has connections with them. It is worth trying.

Ben: In that case, Mary would you please ask him to help out? If I can get Fay back safe and sound, I would be happy to give him a red envelope to show my gratitude.

Mary: Dear cousin Ben, What number are we talking about now?

Ben: (think a second) How about ten million.

Mary: Good, let me give it a shot, I'll get back to you.

Ben: In that case, our hopes all rely on you now.

Mary: It is all in the family, don't worry, I'll do my best.
(Mary leaves, Ted sees her off)

Ben: Dear lord, I hope that I can get my daughter back, I really don't give a damn about the money, I just want my baby saved.

Ted: Dad, you haven't slept for three days, why don't you go lie down and get some rest. I will stay here and watch the phone for you.

Ben: Thank you, I want to, but I can't, how can I get any rest now?

(Shane comes in with a basket full of things from the market)

Shane: Sir, Mrs. Sanders is not back yet?

Ted: No,

Shane: (looks at the table with the food untouched) Sir, You can't just not eat anything at all.

Ben: I have no appetite, I don't want it, please take it away, clear it.

Shane: Yes, sir. (As she starts to clear the table, a car outside honks its horn)

Ben: (excited) It must be your mother, hurry up, Ted, go get the door.

Ted: (rushes to the door) Yeah, it sounds like our car.

(Ted brings Sandy in who looks exhausted, weak and on the edge of crying. followed by the chauffeur with a communications device in hand)

Ben: Sandy, are you all right? You look terrible, what happened? Did you drop off the money?

Sandy: (Weakly) Yes, we did. I have trouble breathing and I don't feel well. I better go lie down for a while.

Ben: Ted, take your mother to her room please. Her heart condition is not that good. We don't want a heart attack on our hands.

Ted: Come on Mom, let's go and get some rest.  (picks up his mother's arm and leads her towards upstairs)

Ben: Juan, please tell me how did you do it?

Juan: First, we circled all over the city while they kept changing the drop off location.  Finally, three hours later, they told us on the walkie talkie to drop the money off at the telephone pole near the turnpike exit.  Right after we dropped off the bag of money, we left for home.

Ben: By now, they should have gotten the money already.  When will they release Fay?

Juan: They said, three hours after they safely got the money, they guaranteed to release Miss Fay.

Ben: I can only hope they will keep their word.

Juan: Sir, will you need me to drive you to office today?

Ben: No, I am not going in today.  You better get something to eat and rest too, God knows what else we have to do.

Juan: Yes, sir, thank you.  (Juan off stage)

Ted: (Ted comes downstairs) Mom is settled down now, Dad, why don't you get some sleep yourself?

Ben: Yes, I am going.  you stay here and watch the phone and take care things.  (gets up and goes upstairs)

Ted: Don't worry Dad, I'll be here.

(Sam comes in from outside)

Ted: Sam, how come you are home so early, your school is not out yet.

Sam: I don't feel well, I got excused from school.

Ted: Are you O.K.?

Same: I arn all right. Is Fay home yet?

Ted:  No, not yet.

Same:  I am going to take a nap, Don't wake me up for lunch.  (Walks toward his room)

Ted:  OK   (Ted sits down, lights a cigarette, reads newspaper, then the phone rings)

Ted:  Yes, speaking, hi, Lily, how are you,.......no, I still can't .......I told you.........Don't get mad, I can't help it either.......I know it is your birthday, I'll make up to you...........I really can't........ My sister is not home yet..........Hello, hello.......... darn it, she hung up. ( gets mad and slams down the phone. Ted walks back and forth, restlessly thinking. As soon as Shane shows up, Ted gladly gets hold of her)

Ted:  Shane, are you going to be around for a while?

Shane:  Yes, what is it?

Ted:  I have to go out for something very important.  If Dad comes down and asks about me, just tell him that I don't fell well, that I am going to the Doctors.

Shane:  Yes, I will.  Ted, are you really sick?

Ted:  No, I am not sick, it is a excuse.  Don't tell any one, OK?  I am on my way.  (Ted heads towards the front door)

Shane:  (Yells out to him)  Will you be back for lunch?

Ted:  Maybe, maybe not, I don't know.  (Ted off stage)

Shane:  I bet he is going to see his girlfriend now.  (Shane off stage)

(Stage is vacant for a moment, Sam comes out of his room with a cup in his hand, into living room pours himself a cup of water.  His hands are shaking, before reaching his mouth spills water all over, then drops the cup on the floor.  He looks at his hands, his whole body shakes, sneezing..........)

Sam:  Oh,what's happening?  My head, oh I feel miserable........ Oh, I can't stand this.

30

Shane: (Comes on stage, looks at Sam) What's the matter with you, Sam? Are you sick?

Sam: Who says that I am sick, I am fine.

Shane: Why are you so pale, you are sneezing and shaking like a leaf, the weather is not that cold yet.

Sam: I have a headache, go away don't bother me.( Turns away from her, holding his head in pain) Oh, it is so hard to get rid of it. (starts to hit himself)

Shane: Sam, Don't do that. What is wrong with you? You look like you are in such pain, let me call the doctor for you.

Sam: No, I am not sick, you don't have to call the doctor.......(starts sneezing and falls on the floor, struggles to get up) I can't take this any more. Oh, my head hurts, my stomach hurts, my whole body hurts...........Shane, please go get me some medicine. I can't take it any more, I think I am going to die.

Shane: Yes, Sam, I'll go to the drug store to get you something for your cold.

Sam: No, it is not for my cold, and you can't get it from the drug store either. I need the drug to fix this, to save my life, I am worse than dead now.

Shane: Are you saying............that you are addicted to drugs? What kind? amphetamines, crack. or what.... tell me.

Sam: It's morphine, heroin.

Shane: Oh, Lord have mercy on you, at your young age, you got hooked on hard drugs. Where can I get it for you?

Sam: In the street beyond the fish market there is a garage, behind it there is a Tobacco shop. There is a guy behind the counter with a tattoo on his left hand. When you see him, you show your thumb and index finger to form the shape of a gun, he will take care of you, it is two thousand dollars for a pack. hurry up. Is that clear to you?

Shane: Gee, that is expensive!

Sam: Hurry up, I am miserable, I am going to die . Oh, I didn't know it would be this bad when I couldn't get a fix.

Shane: How did you ever get started?

Sam: My friends, they told me to try it for fun, who knows I would get hooked. go, go, hurry up.

Shane: OK I am on my way. where is the money?

Sam: I don't have it now. Would you pay for it first? When I see Mom later, I'll ask her to pay you back.

Shane: Alright, I am going.

(Sandy comes out of her room and listens to their conversation, but they are not aware of it)

Sam: Hurry back,I don't know how long I can stand it, and don't let anyone know about this. Do you hear?

Shane: I hear you.

Sam: If Mom knows about this I will never have any peace.

Shane: OK Say no more, I understand.

(Sandy yells to stop her, and quickly comes down the stairs)

Sandy: Shane, where are you going?

Shane: (surprised) I....I...I am going to get medicine for Sam.

Sandy: What kind of medicine?

Sam: The special kind. Mom, can't you see that I have a running nose, have broken out in a cold sweat. My head hurts so much, I feel as if I am going to die. Mom let Shane go now.

Sandy: Sam, You really think you can get away with this, don't you? I overheard your conversation, you are hooked on drugs, am I correct?

Sam: (with shame) Mom.......

Sandy: Sam, how could you? At your young tender age get hooked
on such deadly things....... If your father finds out, how
disappointed he will be. He might even be mad enough to
throw you out of the house.

Sam: Mom, I am so sorry. I know it is wrong, that is why I am trying to
quit. who could know it would get this miserable.

Sandy: I did notice that the last two days you looked awful. I thought
you might have come down with something. I can't imagine
you're addicted to heroin. If you don't get rid of it immediately,
you are wasting your life away, do you know that?

Sam: Say no more, Mom. Why don't you just get a knife and kill me
right now to end my misery. I am in such pain, I would rather die
now. (Squats down holding his head, twitching, his body
shakes all over)

Sandy: (Holding on to Sam) Sam, my baby, I am saying it for your own
good, Alright, as long as you are in such pain, Shane, go get
him a package, now. Tomorrow I'll check you into the
rehabilitation center, to get rid of this dreadful habit.

Shane: Yes, Ma'am. (Shane runs out)

Sam: (Screaming) Hurry, my life depends on it.

Sandy: Oh, my baby, it is all my fault. I didn't protect you well enough.
It hurts me more, to see you suffer like this........ those evil
people use drugs to murder the young and innocent kids. God
help me, please have mercy on us.

(Ben in his robe, comes out of the room, hears her and is on his way
down while talking)

Ben: Dear, who are you talking to? What's going on? You woke me up;
did they release Fay?

Sandy: I am sorry, I didn't mean to wake you up. Fay is not back yet.
Sam didn't feel well, we were arguing over whether he should
go to the doctor. I sent Shane to get some medicine for him.
Nothing else.

Ben: Oh, by the way, Sam, I saw your report card for this term. You are not doing very well, do you want me to find you a tutor?

Sam: No, thank you Dad. I really feel sick, I am going to my room now.

Ben: Go ahead. ( turns to Sandy) Dear, do you think that we ought to have a doctor come and take a look at him?

Sandy: No, I don't think so, the medicine is coming, after he takes that, he will be alright. Don't worry.

Ben: (sighs) Hi, by now, it is more than three hours after you dropped off the money, why isn't Fay home yet? What if they got the money and are not keeping their word? Then all our efforts were wasted.

Sandy: I have the feeling that maybe we should listen to Ted. Those devils are too untrustworthy. I am scared.

Ben: Where is Ted? (Calls out for him, goes to Ted's room, checks, closes the door again) I asked him to stay put, now he is out again, you just can't count on him.

(Juan brings Fay in from outside, Fay wears the same clothing, with some rips. she appears to be in shock, walks in a daze and is almost motionless)

Juan: I saw a cab drop miss Fay off at the entrance to our lane while I was polishing the car.

Sandy: Oh, my baby. (holds her and starts to cry)

(Fay is motionless, until her mother holds her, then seems aware of her surroundings and starts to cry in a painful loud voice)

Fay: Mom, oh, Mom.

Sandy: Oh, I am so happy to see you alive. Don't cry, every thing will be fine, Mom is here for you. Oh, my sweet baby.

Ben: Those criminals at least have the decency to keep their word. Tell me what did they put you through? (Starts walking toward her and reaches his hands out for her)

34

Fay: (Backs away from him, hides behind her mother and breaks out in hysteria) You stay away from me, get away, get away, I'll kill you........(screams and cries)   (Father is shocked, stops and shakes his head)

Sandy: (Holds on to her and pats her on the back,to calm her down) Fay, stop, he is your father, look at him, he is Dad.  You are safe now, hush, hush.  I am here, I am here.

Ben: What have they done to you? poor thing.  Don't worry, you are home now.  look at the room, the sofa, the chair, look around, this is your home.  you are safe, your are safe.  Do you understand?

(Fay gradually stops crying and starts to look around, gradually finds the surroundings familiar,  looks at her father and recognizes him, throws herself on her father, calls out Dad then starts to cry again.  Everyone shows various emotions)   I am glad that you are home and safe, baby.

Sandy:  Ben, She is still upset, let me take her to get some rest first. we'll talk later.  You all can relax now.

Ben: Alright, baby, I'll see you later.  (gives her to Sandy, both of them head to Fay's room while Shane bring Mr. Young in)

Shane:  Sir, Mr. Young is here to see you.

Ben:  Oh, how are you Mr. young?  (shake hands with each other) Come, sit down please.

Shane:  Thank goodness, Miss Fay is home.

Sandy:  Yes, she is exhausted, I am taking her for some rest.  by the way, did you get the medicine for Sam yet?

Shane:  I did, here it is.  (shows Sandy the drug)

Ben:  What kind of medicine is it, let me see.  (reaches his hand out for it)

Sandy:  (waves her arm, signalling Shane to leave)  It is a special formula from the drug store for colds.   Shane, hurry up, take it to Sam,

tell him take it with a lot of water to relieve those symptoms, I know he will feel better soon. Ben, you have a guest, I won't bother you. Mr. Young, please excuse us. (Shane runs first to Sam's room, followed by Sandy holding on to Fay toward Fay's room)

Young: Yes, by all means. Don't mind me.

Ben: (Pouring a glass of water for Mr. Young) Mr. Young, excuse us, I am not shaved and dressed. It has been like hell the last three days.

Young: I am so sorry to hear about your ordeal. Shane told me about it on my way in.

Ben: She was kidnapped three days ago, you can imagine what we have been through. They just released her. She still is in shock from the trauma, poor thing.

Young: You and Mrs. Sanders have been the most kind people, the good Lord will always be on your side. I am sorry that you had to pay a ransom to get her back.

Ben: I didn't mind the ransom. I was afraid they would take the money and still kill her. Now-a-days, any kind of thing can happen.

Young: Yes, I am afraid so. The good economy has brought a great deal of money to the nation; it has also brought a great deal of social problems. The new rich don't know how to handle sudden wealth, the young ones don't have the proper guidelines to follow. People became so materialistic, they forgot the old values and subtleties. If they don't have it, they will break the law to get it. I think the new rich have not learned the social consciousness yet. It will need a great deal of time and education for all of us to learn how to cope with this social problem.

Ben: I agree, I wish more people would listen to you. Now what can I do for you? Do you need more money for your program?

Young: No thank you, not today. I am here this time for a different purpose. As you know, the last few months we were working on the expansion and renovating. Due to your generosity it is almost complete. Next month, on the fifth, we are going to

3 6

have a ceremony to commemorate the use of the new building; this is the invitation.

Ben: (takes a look at the invitation) Next month, on the fifth..........

Young: Yes, I represent the children of our Orphanage who are inviting you to cut the ribbon for our new building, which you so generously donated.

Ben: Oh, no, You should be the one to cut the ribbon. You have devoted your whole life for those children.

Young: Frankly, without you, no matter how hard we worked, it would never have gotten so far. Therefore you should have the honor to lead our celebration.

Ben: Thank you, I am really honored. However, I have scheduled a business trip to go abroad, and I don't know for sure that I'll be back by the fifth. I can't promise you.

Young: Where are you going?

Ben: To Thailand. I have some business to do there, and also want to see some relatives and old friends. I tell you what, if I make it back on time, I'll cut the ribbon, if not, you'll do the honor.

Young: Great, let's just plan on that. Oh, there is something else that I want to discuss with you. The social service bureau has asked us to nominate the most charitable person of the year. In order to publicly thank you for your contribution, may we give them your name this year? Please don't turn us down again like in the past.

Ben: I have told you over and over again, I don't want people to know what I enjoy doing. This is my contribution to put back into my community, I can't accept any public acknowledgement.

Young: Ben, You are too modest and too humble.

Ben: No, it is not that. I have been blessed with good fortune and loving family. What I give is just to pay back what society has given me. I really wish to keep anonymous. If you insist on going public, then I will not give any more.

Young: By all means we respect your wish. I just feel that you deserve to be recognized.

Ben: I truly appreciate your feelings. Tell you the truth, it is a joy for me to give, I get such a pleasure out of it. I am not worth being glorified.

Young: In that case, I will not impose on you. You have my utmost admiration.

Ben: Thank you, I certainly appreciate your good will, and admire your dedication. Your love is the best thing that has happened to those children.

Young: Thank you, I better get going, I'll see you soon.

Ben: Goodbye, keep up with the good work!

( Young off stage from the front door)

Ben: Shane.....

Shane: (Comes out from Sam's room) Yes, Sir?

Ben: Will you please make me a cup of coffee. I'll be in the study.

Shane: Yes, Sir.

(Shane makes coffee at one of the cupboards, Ben turns on the light in the study, opens the safe, gets out papers and begins carefully reading. Shane brings in the the coffee, comes out, then straightens out the living room. Ben lights a pipe, sips coffee while reading. The door bell rings, Shane brings in Datsun)

Shane: (Talking as she walks into the living room) Please sit down, let me go tell your uncle that you are here. He is in the study.

Datsun: No, don't bother, I'll go in to see him myself. (Datsun walks into study) Hi, Uncle Ben.

Ben: Great, good to see you, Datsun.

Datsun: How is it going? Is Fay back yet?

(Shane brings in some tea then leaves)

Ben: They just released her a while ago.

Datsun: That's great. As long as she is safe, that's all that matters. We all know, it could been worse.

Ben: Yes, you are right. The people from the States, have they arrived yet?

Datsun: Yes, they are here. They are at the hotel, in their rooms waiting for your decision.

Ben: Before you arrived, I gave some serious thought to this deal. I think I ought to give it up, not touch it.

Datsun: Why, Uncle Ben? The profit is enormous, this is a chance in a lifetime. Overall, this business deal is too good to let go. Why are you thinking of backing off?

Ben: I don't know, I just feel my luck has not been good lately, I am afraid something might go wrong.

Datsun: Uncle Ben, trust me. I am your nephew. I will not get you in trouble. See, here, (gets out a cable) I just got another cable from Los Angeles. They are very sincere and anxious to consummate the deal. (Ben sees the cable, shows more inner struggle and conflict) Datsun, are you sure this deal will bring us three billion in profit?

Datsun: May be more. Uncle Ben, you just lost fifty million over the ransom money. You have to figure out some way to earn it back. As long as we carefully plan everything, nothing will go wrong. Last time we only did a test run, do you remember the profit margin?

Ben: You are right. We must be very careful. We can't afford any carelessness or mistakes. You know I have my reputation to protect. I can't allow any chance to jeopardize my reputation and the business.

39

Datsun: Uncle Ben, don't worry, I am the front, in case of any trouble, I'll be in The United States, What can they do to me. Relax, nothing will go wrong.

Ben: (Still can't make up his mind) You think so?

Datsun: Uncle Ben, time has changed, the current is changing too. You have to change your way of doing business in order to survive.

Ben: Do we really have to change?

Datsun: There is a saying that "you have to be ahead of people and things to be the leader, if you follow behind, you will only get the leftovers"

Ben: Are you leaving tomorrow to go back to the States?

Datsun: Yes, as soon as I get there, I'll call you. With your money and my connections, we'll make it big. We will still fifty-fifty split, right?

Ben: Yes, you go ahead, go talk to Mr. Smith more on the details. I have to take care of a few odds and ends, I'll meet you there.

Datsun: Fine, Uncle Ben, don't think too much. Make up your mind. I'll see you there. (Off stage through the front door)

Ben: Yes, I'll see you later. (puts papers back in the safe, locks it. He paces back and forth. Ben sees Sandy come out of Fay's room painfully crying silently, he rushes out of the study)

Ben: Dear, what's wrong? Why are you crying?

Sandy: Oh, My GOD! They ruined our daughter. (breaks out with a loud cry. and runs toward Ben)

Ben: What? Ruined our daughter? (twitches, in pain)

Sandy: Fay told me, after they abducted her, they tied her up, blindfolded her and kept her in a room without any food or water. After a day or so they gave her some bread and juice. She said right after she drank the juice, she lost consciousness.

Ben: They must have drugged her.

Sandy: When she came around, she found herself naked from the waist down. She got hysterical and started to scream; then someone handed back her clothing. From that point on she has not been herself. I think she still has not recovered from the trauma. Ben, those criminals have ruined us all. What are we going to do?

Ben: ( Angrily shouting) Those god dammed animals, the sons of bitches. If I catch them I kill them myself. Oh God, there must be justice some where? Oh, my poor baby.

(Shane rushes in, shocked by the noise)

Shane: What happened? What's going on?

Sandy: Shane, everything is fine, get back to the kitchen, don't mind us here.

(Ben composes himself, looks at his watch, realizes that he has a date)

Ben: Shane, tell Juan to get ready, I am going out.

Shane: Yes, sir. (quickly off stage)

Sandy: Where are you going?

Ben: I am going to meet some Americans for a business meeting. (While he is talking, he changes his clothing, putting on a tie and jacket) I probably will not be home for dinner. Please don't wait for me.

Sandy: What about Fay, what should we do?

Ben: For the time being, not a thing, just keep it quiet to ourselves. She might need some counselling, make sure you stay with her. Dammed things like these make me feel so helpless.

Sandy: We have never done anything to hurt anyone, we try our best to be good. Why should things like this happen to us? (sobs quietly)

41

(Ted comes in from outside)

Ted: Hi, Dad, Mom, is Fay home?

Ben: Yes, she is home, no thanks to you. Where have you been?
When a family has a crisis, how could you just leave, and go out
to have fun with your friends?

Ted: I only stepped out for a short while.........

Shane: Juan is ready for you sir.

Ben: (Toward Ted) You better stay put, don't wander around outside,
next time the kidnapping victim could be you! Goodbye. (off
stage from front door)

Sandy: Your father is right, we better be more careful from now on.
God knows when they are going to strike again.

Ted: I told you that we should have reported it to the police; now we all
have to live under the shadows of the kidnappers. Is Fay in her
room? Let me say hello to her.

Sandy: Leave her alone, she is asleep.

Ted: Mom, let me show you something. A friend of mine just got it for
me.

Sandy: What is it?

Ted: (Ted gets out a handgun) See, I bought a gun, for self defense.
From now on I don't have to be afraid of being kidnapped any
more.

Sandy: What, you bought a gun?

Shane: Oh! a gun, where did you get it? Is it expensive?

Sam: (Comes out of his room, looking much better) What, Ted, you
got a gun? Is it a toy gun or the real thing?

Ted: Of course it is a real gun. It's also loaded with bullets, this is no
joke.

Sam: Let me see it.

( Fay quietly opens her door and listens to them; no one sees her)

Ted: You may take a look, but don't touch the trigger. If it's fired accidentally, we will all be in trouble.

(Ted hands to Sam. While Sam is looking at it, Fay quietly walks toward Sam and stares at the gun)

Fay: Ted, May I take a look at your gun?

Ted: Sure, you just be careful.

( Sam gives the gun to Fay, she holds it in her hand and stares at it)

Ted: I am glad that you are home. How did they treat you?

(The question triggers Fay's thoughts, and she starts to show pain and slowly points the gun toward her head)

Fay: They ruined my life. They might as well have killed me; there is no way that I can live any more. I want to die.

Sandy: Fay, please don't........Baby, baby listen to me, we all love you so much, there are so much to live for.

Fay: No...... not for me, I don't want to live any more.

Sandy: Fay......Fay.... just think, you have a nice family, we are all here for you, we are going to pull through this. You are going to be fine.

Fay: I can't....... not after what they did to me........(in tears, shakes her head)

Sandy: (In tears, begging) Let the past go! Baby you've got the future ahead of you. Please, if you die, there is no way that I can live, Please, please give me the gun. Yes, you can do it...... yes......Oh my baby.

(Fay in a daze watches her mother crying, shakes her head and hands over the gun. Sandy holds her tight, both crying out loud)

43

Shane: Shoot! That was close. Miss Fay, You are so lucky to have been born into this family like a princess, you must live and enjoy it.

Ted:  If I knew you were going to do this I would never have even shown you my gun.

Sam:  We all love you; it's a good reason to live.

Lights out and the curtains down, the end of Second Act.

# Act 3

**Time**: One month later.

**Scenery**: Same as Last two Acts.

**Characters**: Same as last two Acts, with the exception of Ben.

## Scene One

(Curtains up, no one is on stage yet. Lights are on. It is about 7:pm. Phone rings, Shane comes from kitchen answers it while Sandy comes out of her room on her way down)

Shane: Ted is not here right now, please call back later, he will be home for dinner. (hangs up the phone)

Sandy: Who was that looking for Ted?

Shane: Some girl named Lou Lou.

Sandy: (sigh) Yeah, if it's not a bar girl, it would be a dance hall girl. Day in, day out he is fooling around, hardly pays any attention to the business. He will not amount to anything useful, I am afraid. (Door bell rings, Shane gets the door and brings Mary in)

Mary: Sandy, is Ben back from Mainland China yet?

(Shane brings tea to Mary, then off stage)

Sandy: He is due back this evening. Juan already left to pick him up at the airport; he should be here soon. Where have you been, I haven't seen you for about a month. What are you up to?

Mary: I have been busy with the stock market. At first, it was good, I made quite a killing. Lately, the world economy has been more

45

unstable, the market has dropped so low, it's almost cleaned me out.

Sandy: Oh, that's too bad.

Mary: That's why I am here. I want to borrow some money from you. Do you have some on hand?

Sandy: How much do you need?

Mary: How about two million?

Sandy: (Shocked) You want to invest this large an amount?

Mary: No, I am considered a small account; some of my friends play in hundreds of millions.

Sandy: I don't have that much cash on hand. I'll ask Ted to write you a check. He should be home soon.

Mary: That's fine. Please don't let my cousin Ben know about this. Otherwise, I will not have peace and quiet from him.

Sandy: Yes, I know.

Mary: By the way, how is Fay doing now? Is she getting any better.

Sandy: She is better, but she still has ups and downs. What kind of curse this is. Poor thing, she is the sweetest one.

Mary: The last twenty years our society has changed so much. Ever since our economy took off, the standard of living rose and so did the crime rate. It seems so easy to make money, people became so ostentatious, competing in showing off their wealth. For some who don't have it, they feel it's easy to rob the rich, because the rich have no faith in the authorities. That is the breakdown of our justice system. Do you remember when we were little, we never heard of such crimes as today's. The criminals all have guns, killing people or even police man is no longer a big deal. Isn't it terrible?

Sandy: I know, and the worst one I think is the using of drugs. All kinds of them, the kids get hooked, then they are as good as dead.

So many of them have tried, but still couldn't kick the habit. I think we need a better program or something.

Mary: I heard that Sam has that problem, is it true?

Sandy: (sigh) As the saying goes " The good things never get out of the front door, yet the bad things travel thousands of miles" Mary, where did you hear this?

Mary: From my son, in school. He told me that there are quite a few of them. Some kids even make money to satisfy their habit by selling it to their classmates.

Sandy: I can't believe that school kids do this. I know there has been a sharp decline of discipline, respect, and ethics, but I never imagined that it was this bad. I guess some kids watch their parents in action with money and they become materialistic too. Greed is the major cause of the breakdown of the family life and morality.

Many: Today's young people are more sophisticated than we used to be. They have more needs, but they have no proper place to go for properly guided social activities. There are not enough sports activities to keep them busy. The good students need all the time to study, but for those who have enough of school work, there are not enough extra curricular things for them to channel their energy. I am surprised that we don't have more problems than what we already have.

Sandy: I think you are right. Ben doesn't know about it yet. I don't want to hurt him while he is so busy. I sent Sam to the Recovery and Treatment Center last month, while his father was away. Hopefully he is cured by now, and everything will be fine.

Mary: I sure hope so. I guess we are all guilty in some ways for giving our children too much. Is this what we have to pay for a higher standard of living? Is this really worth it?

Sandy: I don't know, I guess as adults, we constantly have to educate ourselves to face the changing of the times and the problems that come with prosperity. I feel that unless we learn how to deal and cope with it, we are going to lose the battle, and lose

our children as well. Most times I really don't know what to do. I wish I were better prepared.

(Ted walks in from the front door)

Ted: Hi Mom, hi, Aunt Mary. How are you today? Mom, is Dad home yet?

Sandy: No, not yet. We were talking while waiting for him.

Ted: (Looking at his watch) He should be home by now. It is almost eight o'clock.

Sandy: Maybe they got caught in the speedway rush hour. Ted, would you please write a check for the amount of two million for your Aunt Mary. She needs it before your father gets home.

Ted: Sure, Mom. (Ted gets the checkbook) Aunt Mary, do you want your name on it or just Cash?

Mary: Just cash, it is for tomorrow.

Ted: (Finishes writing, hands to Mary) You better take good care of it. this way anybody can cash it.

Mary: Thank you, Ted. Sandy, I'll pay you back next month. I better get going now.

Sandy: Aren't you going to wait for you cousin and stay for dinner?

Mary: No, thank you, I better go home and check on the kids, I have not seen them all day. I wonder what they up to? (Mary sees herself out)

Fay: ( Fay comes out of her room talking at the same time) Mom, where is Dad? I am hungry.

Sandy: Dear, why don't you get yourself something to eat first. Yesterday he sent me a telegram saying that the flight should get him home in time for dinner. He said there are presents for every one, especially for you, Fay. It is getting late, I hope nothing happened during the flight.

Fay: No, Mom, It can't be. How could you think of such thing?

Sandy: Last night, I had a strange dream. I dreamed of your father
waved to me and said goodbye. I got frightened and woke up.
I think this is a bad omen.

Fay: Mom, Dad is very healthy. He is so kind and sweet, nothing bad
will happen to him.

Sandy: Then, why isn't he home? Maybe they were in a car accident.
Tomorrow is his birthday, He promised me that he will be home
for the party, you heard him too, didn't you?

Fay: Yes, Mom, calm down. Everything will be fine. Doesn't Juan
know, in case of delay or anything like that he should give us a
call, so that we won't worry?

Sandy: He should, but sometimes he doesn't use his head.

(Door bell rings)

Sandy: Shane, hurry up, open the door. It must be them.

(Shane gets the door, Datsun follows her in, he looks troubled and is in
a rush)

Sandy: Hi, Datsun, did you just come from the States?

Datsun: Yeah........Aunt Sandy, is Uncle Ben home?

Sandy: No, not yet. We are waiting for him. We are kind of worried, he
is very late by now.

Datsun: Aunt Sandy, I am in a hurry. I have to take care of a few things
before leaving for the States first thing in the morning. I can't
wait.

Sandy: You just got here, and you are leaving again?

Datsun: (speaks fast) Yes, when Uncle Ben is home, tell him that the
shipment I brought in from the U.S. has arrived. However the
container has been impounded by customs. If they want to
open and search it, we may have some trouble on our hands.
Tell him to find someone to take care of it. I've got to go; after I
reach back to States, I'll call him. Tell him don't even try to reach

49

me. Goodbye Ted, goodbye Fay, take good care of yourself kid.

(Datsun rushs off stage)

Sandy: What's matter with that kid, he acts like as if his tail is on fire.

Fay: Mom, Datsun said that Dad's cargo is impounded by customs; we might have some trouble. Dad's cargo is antiques; what kind of trouble could it be?

Sandy: Don't worry, your father will take care of it.

Ted: That's strange, I didn't know that you can import large amount of antiques.

(Door bell rings, Shane rushes to the door and brings Sam in)

Fay: Sam, I thought you were not allowed to come home while at the treatment center; are you all finished and well?

Sam: No, I am not done yet, but I can't stand it any more, I am running away from there.

Sandy: Running away? You quit? Don't you want to get rid of it?

Sam: Mom, that place, they locked me up in my room, as if I were a criminal. It drove me crazy. I've got to get away from that forsaken place. Shane, please go get me some more of that medicine, I am about due for a fix now.

Ted: The way you are acting, you'll never recover from it.

Sam: Shane, would you please hurry up.

(Shane looks at Sandy, to get her opinion)

Sandy: Don't go, see what he is going to do!

Sam: Mom are you really this vindictive? You really want to see me roll on the floor? Alright, if you all going to be so mean, I might as well leave you all and go kill myself in some alley. (Sam turns around to leave, Shane stops him)

Shane: Sam, don't act like this, we only want the best for you. We are doing it for your own good.

(Sam starts to have withdrawal symptoms of pain and agony)

Sam: (On his knees begging) Mom please, help me, I can't stand it. Oh........Oh.........I am going to die...........

Fay: Mom, just help him this once.

Ted: Mom, you have to do it this time, we will figure out some way to deal with him later.

Sandy: Alright, Shane, you go and get him a package. Oh, God, what's happening to us ? (crying)

(Shane off stage)

Sandy: Fay, bring your brother to his room. Don't let your father come home and sees him in this mess. It will hurt him deeply.

(phone rings, Ted picks it up)

Ted: Yes, Juan......(talks to Sandy) It is Juan from the airport.

Sandy: Let me talk to him. (Takes the phone) Yes, what..... what did you say?

Juan: (Stage sound system amplifies the phone conversation) Madam, Master's plane from Bangkok, Thailand to Hong Kong has crashed . I am waiting to confirm his name from the passengers' list.

Sandy: Yes, Juan you wait there, to make sure. If there is any news, please call. (Sandy in shock, drops the phone, almost passes out, Ted picks up the phone and holds on to his mother with Fay to comfort her)

Fay: (scared) Mom, Calm down, Dad might not even have been on that flight. Please don't cry. ( Fay starts to cry and curls up into a withdrawal position rocking back and forth like a baby)

Ted: Mom, don't worry, Dad is a good person, he will not die like this.

Sandy: Ben, we have been so good, God will not take you away like this...........(crying out)

Lights out. End of scene one.

## Scene Two.

When the lights gradually turn on, there is sad music in the
        background.
The living room has an altar set up.  On the wall, above the altar is Ben's
        enlarged picture. On the table are flowers, white candles, fruits
        and an incense burner.  In front of it on the floor is a bucket,
        Shane is burning paper money in it.  Juan is lighting the
        candles and incense.


Juan: I just can't believe that he is gone.  What a shame, we all going to
        miss him.

Shane: I can't even dream of such a thing.  It all happened so fast.
        Madam said that she had a dream the night before it happened.
        Mr. Sanders was waving to her goodbye.  I can't believe that
        her premonition came true.

Juan: there are plenty of things that are unbelievable.  Do you
        remember how many friends our master used to have?   After
        he died, have you noticed any one been around?

Shane: Don't talk about it any more, it is so depressing.

Juan: OK I won't say any more.   Oh, it is about time for me to pick Miss
        Fay up from her school.  Ever since her father passed away,
        Miss Fay has not been doing well, I hope there are no more
        accidents.

Shane: What do you mean, by accidents?  You mean she might try to
        kill herself again?

Juan: May be, you better keep an eye on her, watch her closely.  Our
        Mistress could no longer face another tragic incident.

Shane: I know.  You better go.

(Door bell rings)

Juan: Let me get it for you, I'll go out that way. See you later. ( Juan goes out through the front door, and in comes Mr. Young.)

Shane: How are you Mr. Young. Please sit down, I'll go to get Mrs. Sanders for you.

( Mr. Young sits down, Shane goes upstairs, Sandy follows her down. Sandy is in mourning cloth. Shane brings tea from off stage)

(Mr. Young bows to Sandy then goes in front of Ben's picture and bows deeply three times, Sandy bows back)

Sandy: Mr. Young, what can I do for you?

Young: Not a thing, I am here to pay a tribute to an old friend. The children at the Orphanage all were very saddened by the loss of your husband. . Please accept our condolences. Please be strong and take good care of yourself. May peace be with you.

Sandy: Thank you, You have all been very kind.

Young: We were all shocked by the news. Tragic accidents happen to the kindest people, it seems not quite fair. Sometimes we just have to have faith and keep believing that there is more than we can see.

Sandy: Yes, I begin to think so. The last few days I have thought about it over and over. I gave up fighting against the inevitable, I surrender myself to fate. I think it is meant to be this way.

Young: I don't think it is meant to be this way at all. I think the good Lord is calling him for some other important mission. I can't get used to the idea that he is gone, I am going to miss him.

Sandy: We all do. We also have to carry on our duties, right?

Young: To hear you talking like this, I am relieved. I think you are going to do just fine.

Sandy: I have no choice. If it is not for Ben, just for our children, I have to be strong. There are a great deal of things that need to get done. Your children for instance, I will never desert them. Please continue to count on my support.

Young: Madam, I don't know what to say, from the bottom of my heart, may God be with you.

Sandy: Don't say anything. This is my commitment.

Young: I am going to leave now, please get some rest and take care.

Sandy: Shane, Please see Mr. Young out.

Shane: Yes, Madam.

(Shane follows Young to the front door. Just as she is about to come in, the doorbell rings again, she returns to the door and brings Mary in. Mary goes and bows three times to Ben's picture, Sandy returns with one bow, then they hug each other)

Mary: How could he leave us like this, without any warning. I loved him like my own brother. (she starts to cry)

Sandy: Don't cry, otherwise you are going to get me started all over again.

Mary: OK I'll stop, I don't think you can take it any more. Is Ted back?

Sandy: Yes, He brought back Ben's ashes last night. They are out looking for a burial plot.

Mary: Sandy, the money I borrowed from you, will due soon, but I have had trouble putting my money together. Will you give me more time? All my money is tied up in the stock market.

Sandy: Of course, take your time, I don't need it right now.

Mary: Sandy, your are really the sweetest person, you have always helped me out, whenever I needed you.

Sandy: Don't be silly, we are family.

Mary: There is an article in the newspaper, I don't know whether you have seen it or not? (Gets out a copy of the paper to show to Sandy)

Sandy: What article? Let me read it.

(music becomes strong and emotional)

Sandy: What happened? Datsun was arrested at the airport when he was leaving for The States.

Mary: Is this true or not? I can't believe it.

Sandy: (continues reading) The cargo of the container which was shipped from The States, was searched by the customs officials. They concluded that only a small amount of it was antiques as claimed. The majority of the cargo was arms and ammunition, including a large number of automatic machine guns.

Mary: I can't believe that Ben would do such a thing. May be there is some kind of mix up in the information.

Sandy: Oh, my God, they also found a large quantity of heroin and crack cocaine. (Puts down the paper) This can't be true, Ben was a law abiding business man, he wouldn't have done this. It is impossible.

Mary: I can't believe this either, that's why I am here to ask you.

Sandy: (Looks confused) Ben did make a lot of money in the last few years. He said the economy was great for the import and export business.............. Could it possibly be the devil's business?

Mary: Look here, another article says that at the conclusion of the investigation, Datsun admitted all the wrong doing. He stated that the person in charge who financed the whole thing was his uncle.

Sandy: Stop it, say no more...... Datsun knows that his uncle is dead and defenseless, it would be easy to blame it all on a dead person. Oh, my headache is back again, Shane, please get me the ointment for my head.

Shane: Yes madam. (Puts it on Sandy's temple)

Mary: I've got something else to do, I better go, I'll call you some other day. I'll see myself out. (Mary rushes off stage from the front door)

(Sandy sits down carefully reading the articles again, the microphone records her thoughts)   No wonder the last few years Ben was anxious to do charity work, to give, to contribute. I bet, he just wanted to ease his conscience. Let me open his safe to see whether I can find more evidence to prove my suspicion.

(Sandy goes into the study, turns on the light, opens the safe.  There are money, gold bullion and documents. she carefully searches for clues)

Sandy:  What it this , a copy of a contract. He is going to buy .......oh, my God, heroin, cocaine, and ..........ammunition. They are going to split the profit fifty-fifty.  Ben, what have you done, Oh God, how could you do this. Oh, what am I going to do? (cries out loud and tears up the contract.)

(Sam comes in from outside, sees the study light on, and comes directly in.  sees the money, his eyes light up)

Sam:  Mom, are you taking count of Dad's stuff?   (Sandy doesn't answer him; he looks at the gold and money)  Wow, a lot of money.  Give me some, I can start a business. (reaches out for it)

Sandy:  (Stops him)  Don't touch, that's to pay for your father's funeral.

Sam:  Just some.  I am not asking for much, I don't want the whole thing.

Sandy:  Give you the money?  So you can get more drugs, right?

Sam:  Mom, trust me, I'll kick the habit soon.  I talked with my friends, we are going to be in business together.  I need money to start, If you won't give me the cash, the gold bullion will do.

Sandy:  You liar, How did I give birth to such a scum bag. Get out, get out you miserable useless fool.

(Ted comes in from outside, looks tired and sad.  hears the noise, comes to the study)

Ted: Mom, we selected Dad's burial ground already. Sam, what are you arguing about?

Sandy: He wants me to give him money to starts a business. I refused.

Ted: Don't be ridiculous, you are still in school.

Sam: I want to be independent.

Ted: You get rid of your addiction first. I can't see a drug addict being independent.

Sam: I don't care what you think, never mind my business, let me tell you, Dad is dead now. I want to divide up everything, I want my share of inheritance. From now on, I disown you all.

Sandy: Sam, Your father just died, how can you talk like this?

Ted: I won't allow it either.

Sam: I don't care whether you allow it or not, I am going to get myself a lawyer. (grabs some money and runs)

Sandy: (sigh) I can't believe Sam turned out like this.

Ted: Mom, It is the drug, all the addicts would kill for a fix. As soon as he is cured, he will be fine. (suddenly holds his chest) Mon, I don't feel well, I better go lie down.

Sandy: Since your father died, you have been taking care of everything. you have been working too hard, please go get some rest. ( She touches his forehead, surprised) You are running a fever, do you want the doctor to take a look at you?

Ted: No, there is no need, lately it has been like this, as soon as I get some sleep, I'll be fine.

Sandy: Go ahead. (She puts things back in the safe, closes it and turns off the light outside of the study. Just as she is about to go upstairs, a car horn sounds outside. Shane comes out to open the door; Sandy waits for Fay)

Shane: It is Miss Fay home. (follows Fay in, Fay's eyes are red, she has been crying) What's the matter Miss Fay, what are you crying about?

Sandy: Sweetheart, tell Mom about it. (reachs out and holds her)

Fay: (Throws herself into Mom's arms and breaks down in tears) Mom, I could no longer face anybody in school any more. I want to die, let me end my miserable life.

Sandy: Stop this nonsense, tell me about it; I'll take care of it.

Fay: Mom, you can't take care of this one. (takes a copy of a newspaper out of her bag shows it to Sandy) Did you read the evening news yet? I can't believe that my father is the world's worst criminal. All my classmates asked me about it. I didn't know what to say, I almost went out of my mind.

Sandy: (crying) Baby, what can I say to you. This is your father's own doing. You ask him yourself, let him answer you............

Fay: Dad, what kind of person are you? You have always been generous, and kind to people. Now you are gone, people accuse you of being the most evil criminal. It that true? Tell me, what are you? The truth, I want the truth. I loved you so much, and I miss you. Tell me, please tell me it's not true. I am only in a dream. come on talk to me, why don't you talk to me? Say something...................(howling)

Sandy: Shane, take her to her room, she is too excited, she might have another nervous breakdown.

Shane: Yes, Madam. Come Miss Fay, come with me (drags Fay to her room)

(Sandy stands in the living room staring into space. The phone rings, she doesn't hear at first, then realizes, and picks up the phone)

Sandy: Yes, I am, who is this? Oh, yes Miss Tina. What? They are gone? What's happening then? Where is the vice president? You want Ted? OK, I'll get him. He'll be there soon. (hangs up the phone, and calls out to Ted's room) Ted, come on out, the general manager and chief controller have taken all the

company's assets and disappeared. It is chaos there; the vice president is holding a meeting and waiting for you...........

Ted: (Comes out of his room weak, shaky) Mom, I am too sick to go.

Sandy: What's happened to you? Oh, dear you look dreadful.........(as Ted is about to pass out) Juan, Juan, come quick.

Ted: Mom, There is something I have kept a secret from you. I am so sorry, I didn't want to hurt you. I am afraid that I won't have much time left to be with you now.

Sandy: Don't talk like that, we all need you now. What is it that you didn't tell me?

Ted: Mom, I have Aids. I got it from the prostitutes. I didn't know that I had to protect myself that way. The doctor said it is in the final stage, it can be any time now. Mom........

Sandy: Aids! Oh, no, my baby.

Juan: ( Just walks in, hears the word aids) Aids, you?

(Ted passes out in Juan's arm)

Lights out, sad music starts while the lights are out. End of scene two.

## Scene Three

Lights gradually turn on, concentrated on the picture on the wall. Sandy sits in a rocking chair thinking motionlessly. The atmosphere is very depressing.

Juan: ( Juan comes in bows to the picture, then faces Sandy)  The cook Leo has left; I am on my way too. I just wanted to say goodbye and thank you for all the years that you all have been so good to me. I am sorry to leave you.

Sandy: Thank you Juan, we had good days didn't we? I am sorry that I couldn't keep you any longer,  there is nothing left.

Juan: I am sorry, Madam. Please take good care of yourself. (quietly off stage from the kitchen)

(Sandy walks toward the picture, stares at it. Sound system amplifies her monolog)

Sandy: Ben, can you see us, are you aware of what has happened? With the crime that you committed, the government seized all that was left that your manager didn't embezzle. All your assets are gone. Ted is in the hospital for his final days, drawing his last breath. Sam was arrested and is in jail for using, possession and dealing drugs. The saddest part, our innocent daughter could not face the humiliation, has withdrow n and hides in her room all day. Oh, what a  way to live her life........(crying)    Every thing is gone, and everybody has left, except Shane. Ben, did you know that your greed would bring us to this? Before you did all that, did you ever think about us? If you truly  loved us you wouldn't have put us in a hell like this. Oh, you ruined us all........(Crying and using her fist hits herself or the wall as the lights dim to minimum)

(Ben' voice on)

Sandy, I am so sorry, Sandy, We did have a good life together. You have been a good wife and mother. I love you, and my family. I let the greed and ego blind me, and brought you such pain and suffering. You have been so good and I let you down  I am so sorry.......

61

Sandy: Sorry, what's the use of being sorry? I want my family back, give me my family...... give it back to me, you hear? (acts crazy) (Shane rushes in and turns on the lights, The stage is back to normal)

Shane: Madam, Why are you in the dark? Who are you talking to?

Sandy: I was talking to Ben, he was here to apologize.

Shane: Madam, Mr. Sanders is dead, please don't torture yourself any more. You have to look after yourself.

Sandy: He is dead, but I was talking to him.

(Shane shakes her head not believing her. The door bell rings. Shane goes to get the door and brings Robert Bond in)

Shane: Madam, here comes the rubber band. (not too loud, Sandy couldn't hear her.

Robert: Ma'am, do you remember me?

Sandy: No, I don't, who are you? What do you want?

Robert: I am Robert Bond........I......I work for the insurance company

Sandy: Oh, yes. You are the one that Shane always teases.

Robert: Yes ma'am. Your husband bought a ten million dollar policy before he left for his trip. I am so sorry about the accident, he was a kind gentleman. According to the contract, you are the beneficiary, I am here to bring you the check. (gets out the check) Please sign here, and this is yours.

Sandy: (can't believe) Is this true?

Shane: Of course it is true. No insurance company will hand out money unless they have to. Hurry up and sign your name, before he changes his mind.

(Sandy signs and takes the check)

Robert: My job is done.  Good luck, Ma'am, Miss.  In.........in the future, if you need..........need insurance, please call me.  this is my name card.

Shane: Hey,  after all, you are not so bad.

Robert: Of course, I am good, I...I work hard, to........to earn a living. I.....I..... only stutter, it doesn't hurt anyone.  Goodbye. (Walking toward front door, Shane follows him to see him off)

Shane: (Comes back toward Sandy)  Ma'am, Life is such a strange thing.  At least you don't have to worry about bread and butter for a while.

Sandy: Yes, you are so right.  Life passes in a mysterious way.  I am afraid, we have a hard time ahead of us.


(A sudden gun shot comes from Fay's room)

Shane: A gun shot, you stay here, don't move, I 'll go and check.  I'll be right back.

(Shane goes into Fay's room.  Screams and shouts)

Shane: Oh, Miss Fay, how could you do this?  Oh, my God!  (As Sandy is about to run in, Shane runs out, crying)  Oh, no, you can't go in there to see her like that.  You can't take it, don't, please don't go in there.  (Pulls Sandy back to the center of the stage)

Sandy: (In shock)  Fay.....My Fay, gun.........Ted's gun.  Fay killed herself with Ted's gun?    No,no...... Ben, do you see what you have done?  ( slowly falls on her knees )  Oh, my God , Ben........  You killed our daughter......( Sandy passes out)


  End of Act three    End of the play